THE BEST AGE EVER*

*results may vary

Crown Publishers
New York

Unless noted below, all photos are courtesy Photofest NYC.
Pages 12–13, 33, 68, 88, 95, 97, 102, 155 © 2004 by Jonathan Van Gieson

Copyright © 2004 by
Joshua Albertson, Lockhart Steele, and Jonathan Van Gieson
Illustrations © 2004 by Jonathan Van Gieson

Published by Crown Publishers, New York, New York.
Member of the Crown Publishing Group, a division of Random House, Inc.
www.crownpublishing.com

CROWN is a trademark and the Crown colophon is a registered trademark of
Random House, Inc.

Printed in the United States

Typeset in Gotham and Hoefler Text
with special appearances by Balmoral, Bamboo, Bubbledot, Emblem, Gill Sans,
Intrepid, and Mansour Contour

Book design by Jonathan Van Gieson
with Joshua Albertson and Lockhart Steele

Steele, Lockhart, 1974–
      The Big 40 : Are You Ready to Face...The Best Age Ever / Lockhart Steele,
Joshua Albertson, Jonathan Van Gieson — 1st ed.
Includes bibliographical references.
1. Middle age. 2. Middle aged persons. I. Title: Big Forty. II. Albertson, Joshua,
1974– III. Van Gieson, Jonathan, 1974– IV. Title.
HQ1059.4.S74 2004
305.244M—dc22   2004055112

ISBN 1-4000-5014-6

10 9 8 7 6 5

First Edition

CONTENTS

"It's weird, when you're 39, it starts to happen..."

—*Keanu Reeves*

A Brief Note About Sources
What you are about to read is real. The data in this book—
no matter how absurd it may seem—
were not fabricated, at least not by the authors.
It comes from a wide variety of sources, ranging from
the U.S. Census to www.howstella.com.
If you don't believe us, read the endnotes.

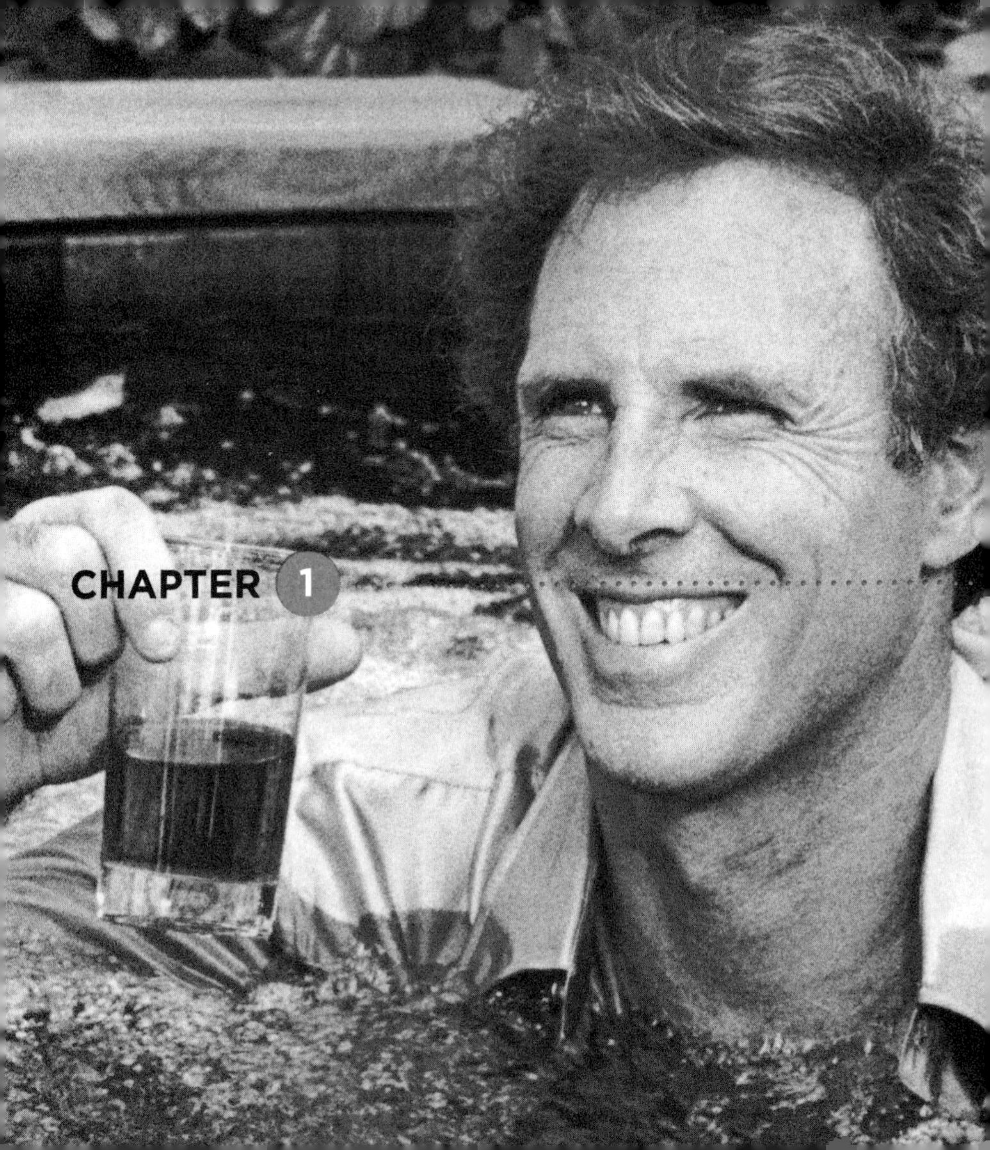

CHAPTER 1

"1. The cardinal number equal to 4 X 10.
2. forties a. A decade or the numbers from
40 to 49: *They stopped smoking in their forties.
At night the temperature fell into the forties.*
b. often Forties. The decade from 40 to 49 in a
century." —*American Heritage Dictionary*

YOU ARE 40

A h, the big 40! Great age. Is it the best ever? Hard to say. Noted philosopher Carl Jung called it the "noon of life." That sounds promising. Then again, sometimes it rains all afternoon. And while some people can sit back at 40 to reflect on all that they've accomplished—the great job, the happy marriage, the overflowing bank account—others can only wonder where it all went so terribly, terribly wrong.

No matter where you stand, *The Big 40!* is here to tell you that you're not alone. We've looked at 40 from inside and out, upside and down. In the pages that follow, we aim not to pass judgment, or to offer soothing bromides, but to uncover what it really means to be 40—the good, the bad, and the Botox.

Will this book make you feel better about your new decade? That's hard to say, too. Does it make you smile to know that Elvis was fat and bloated? Are you saddened by Einstein's success "relative" to yours?

Best Age Ever? Only you can make it so. Or, as our friend Dr. Phil will tell you, "You are a life manager, and your objective is to actively manage your life in a way that generates high-quality results."

40! Live it, love it, embrace it.

A NOTE ABOUT CHAPTER INTRODUCTIONS

Introductions are chock-full of random stuff designed to whet your appetite for the upcoming chapter. The chapter quiz will not be graded.

OMITTED DATA

Data: Number of oranges you would have eaten by age 40 if you had eaten one orange a day
Reason Omitted: Eerily similar to number of apples (p. 13)

Data: 40–49s make up 20% of the US population but 23% of U.S. Internet users
Reason Omitted: Page Not Found

Data: At 40, 30% of men and 20% of women snore regularly
Reason Omitted: Survey conducted in Israel

Data: The median age in Belgium is 40
Reason Omitted: Survey conducted in Belgium

Bonus Data: Dustin Hoffman filmed *The Graduate* at 30.
Reason Included: Meant to put in *Book of Ages 30*, but forgot.

CHAPTER QUIZ

1. What do people do most at age 40?
a. Get promoted
b. Get tattooed
c. Get drunk
d. Get gun

2. TRUE OR FALSE?
The average 40-year-old is more likely to find smoking pot "absolutely wrong" than stealing office supplies.

3. ESSAY QUESTION
You are experienced. Discuss.

WELCOME TO YOUR FORTIES

•••••• **You are now** OLDER **than** 58% of America

Don't worry, you're not alone. 4,511,000 Americans will turn 40 this year

 of Americans are in their 40s

 $22,471 Median income for women at age 40

$38,340 Median income for men at age 40

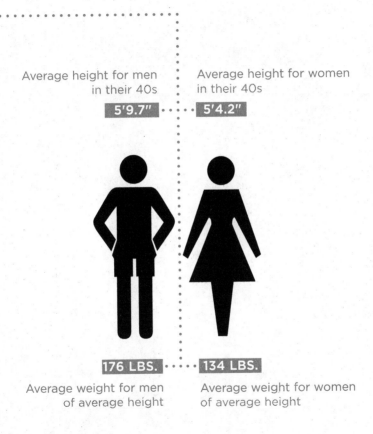

Average height for men
in their 40s

5'9.7"

Average height for women
in their 40s

5'4.2"

176 LBS.

134 LBS.

Average weight for men
of average height

Average weight for women
of average height

feel they are **40%** in excellent health

47% in good health

10% in fair health

3% in poor health

FEELIN' ALRIGHT? **87%** **AIN'T FEELIN' TOO BAD THEMSELVES**
*people in their early 40s
claiming good or excellent health*

IF YOU ATE AN APPLE A DAY **UNTIL YOU TURNED 40**

then

you've

eaten

14,609 APPLES

FORTY IN FORCE

BY 2010 40.6 **WILL BE THE MEDIAN WORKER AGE** · · · · ◂

 34.6 current median worker age

YOU HAVE A **21%** **CHANCE OF** BEING PROMOTED
in the next 5 years

 26% if you have a bachelor's degree

 21% if you have some college but no degree

 21% if you only have a high school diploma

 15% if you have no diploma

 23% if you're a man

20% if you're a woman

BUMMER.  **4.7%** **ARE** UNEMPLOYED
in their early 40s

72% **BELIEVE IN THE DEVIL AND HELL**
in their early 40s

57% believe in ghosts

23% believe in astrology

25% believe in reincarnation

33% attend religious services every week or more

19% a few times a year

18% once a year or less frequently

19% never

81% **BELIEVE IN GOD** *in their early 40s*

33% are absolutely certain

"As you approach 40, you've reached a limit. You start to get permanent changes and decreased ability to repair cartilage and tissue. Tendons are less flexible, so more stretching and warming up is required. Knees are especially vulnerable, as they take a lot of stress from high-impact activit Runners with inherited knock-knees or bowlegs can expect extra pressur and consequent wearing down of bone on the inside or outside of their knee joints and should probably consider lower-impact sports."

—University of Washington Health Bea

DROP AND GIVE ME...

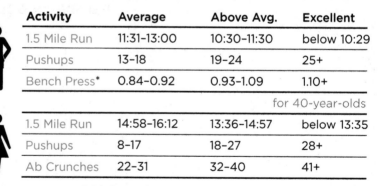

	Activity	Average	Above Avg.	Excellent
	1.5 Mile Run	11:31–13:00	10:30–11:30	below 10:29
	Pushups	13–18	19–24	25+
	Bench Press*	0.84–0.92	0.93–1.09	1.10+
				for 40-year-olds
	1.5 Mile Run	14:58–16:12	13:36–14:57	below 13:35
	Pushups	8–17	18–27	28+
	Ab Crunches	22–31	32–40	41+

*divide heaviest weight you can lift once by body weight

of 40somethings think they are overweight

 feel they are at least 20 percent overweight

of men in their 40s weigh over 232 pounds **10%** of women in their 40s weigh over 209 pounds

Q: Isn't it true that fat people are lazy, stupid, weak-willed, lacking in ambition, selfish, greedy, gluttonous, sedentary, and ugly?

A: No, none of these characterizations have any basis in fact.

—Council on Size & Weight Discrimination FAQ

"My rule of life prescribed as an absolutely sacred rite smoking cigars and also the drinking of alcohol before, after, and if need be during all meals and in the intervals between them." —*Winston Churchill*

BUZZED? **DRANK ALCOHOL IN THE PAST MONTH**
of people in their early 40s

 binged (5 or more drinks on one occasion)

 are heavy drinkers (binged on 5 separate days)

SMOKED? 77% **HAVE SMOKED CIGARETTES**
of people in their early 40s

35% in the past year

32% in the past month

WASTED? 66% **HAVE USED ILLICIT DRUGS**
of people in their early 40s

14% in the past year

8% in the past month

9% have had illicit drug or alcohol dependence or abuse

YOU'RE GETTING · · · · · · · · · · · · · · ·

"Psychological health steadily increases from 30
years of age to 40, 50, and 62 years of age."
—Psychology and Aging, *Vol. 15, No. 2*

People in their early 40s say they are **16%** **extremely** happy

35% **very** happy

31% generally **satisfied**

13% fairly **unhappy**

5% **unhappy** most of the time

· **LESS CRAZY**

"Three-quarters of persons with schizophrenia develop the disease between 16 and 25 years of age. Onset is **uncommon after age 30,** and rare after age 40."

—*Schizophrenia.com*

YOU ARE GUNNIN' FOR TROUBLE ··· **32%** **CARRY A HANDGUN**

3% for work

14% for protection

20% for target

12% for hunting

2% for "other"

24 THE BIG 40!

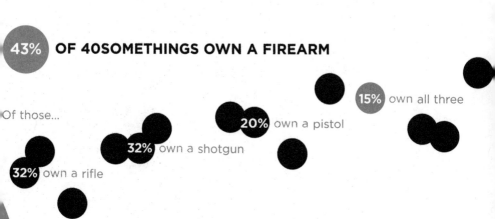

43% OF 40SOMETHINGS OWN A FIREARM

Of those...

32% own a rifle

32% own a shotgun

20% own a pistol

15% own all three

Which of these behaviors do you find  **ABSOLUTELY WRONG?**

	people in their 40s	people in their 30s
lying on your résumé	70%	66%
keeping excess change at the store	70%	63%
cheating the IRS	70%	63%
taking pens and paper from the office	54%	49%

BUT

smoking marijuana	53%	56%

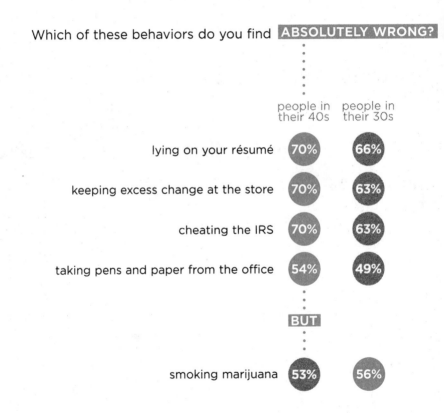

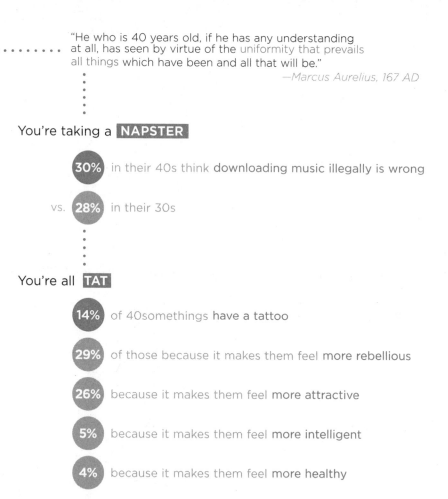

"He who is 40 years old, if he has any understanding at all, has seen by virtue of the uniformity that prevails all things which have been and all that will be."

—*Marcus Aurelius, 167 AD*

You're taking a NAPSTER

30% in their 40s think **downloading music illegally is wrong**

vs. **28%** in their 30s

You're all TAT

14% of 40somethings **have a tattoo**

29% of those because it makes them feel **more rebellious**

26% because it makes them feel **more attractive**

5% because it makes them feel **more intelligent**

4% because it makes them feel **more healthy**

Chances are, if you have not yet realized YOU ARE GAY · · · · · ·

You probably **NEVER WILL**

realized they were gay **2%** after age 40

came out of the closet **4%** after age 40

of people over 40 who
identify themselves as gay

THIRD DEGREE? 26% **HAVE A BACHELOR'S OR HIGHER**
in their 40s

 9% have an advanced degree

 57% have at least some college

85% have a high school diploma

15% have no high school diploma · · · · · · · · · · · ·

"Be wise with speed; a fool at forty is a fool indeed."
—*Edward Young*

•••••• **WAY COOL!** 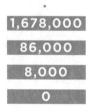 **ARE HEADING BACK TO SCHOOL**
in their early 40s

1,678,000	Early 40s folk are in college
86,000	are in high school
8,000	are in elementary school
0	are in kindergarten or nursery school

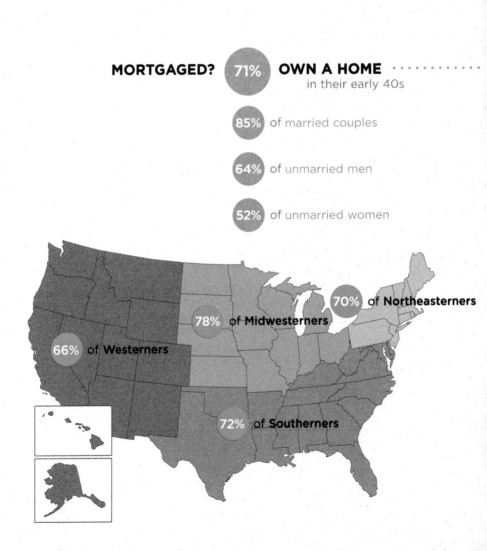

MORTGAGED? 71% **OWN A HOME**
in their early 40s

85% of married couples

64% of unmarried men

52% of unmarried women

66% of Westerners

78% of Midwesterners

70% of Northeasterners

72% of Southerners

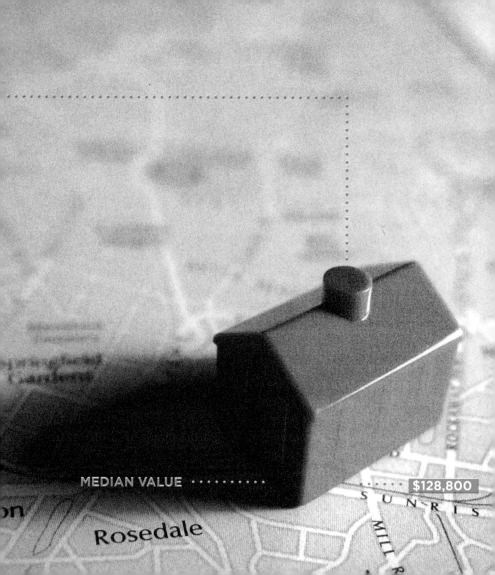

MEDIAN VALUE · · · · · · · · · · $128,800

Rosedale

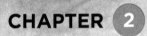

CHAPTER 2

> "Yeah, life begins at forty. Age is just a state of mind."
>
> —*John Lennon, "Life Begins at Forty"*

LIFE BEGINS AT 40

Sobbing over those 40 candles? Bah! What with the average American life expectancy approaching 80 in this country, you're just getting ready for the second half of the "game of life." And as any sports fan knows, nothing really happens until the second half. (Well, nothing really happens until the last five minutes, but that's not going to work here, is it?) For further encouragement, we turn to About.com's beauty editor, who, as always, knows best: "Your life is changing yet again. You are getting older. Is this something that you should be worrying about?

"Worried? Your life is just about to get better. But, you can't let down your guard. There are still some things that you have to do if you don't want to look your age...and who does?"

MOST SHOCKING REVELATION IN THIS CHAPTER

Carol Shields disapproves of "bimbos and bitches." (p. 47)

LEAST SHOCKING REVELATION

Muhammad was bored with his first career, merchant. (p. 41)

FIRST TWO LINES OF THE SECOND VERSE OF THE THEME FROM *THE JEFFERSONS*

Fish don't fry in the kitchen
Beans don't burn on the grill

OMITTED DATA

Data: Reference to "hated" New York Yankees in George Steinbrenner bio
Reason Omitted: Reflects bias of Red Sox–crazed author

Data: Shirley Temple biography
Reason Omitted: Mistakenly began working on *The Big 4!*

Data: Shirley Templeton bio
Reason Omitted: Doesn't exist; product of one author's confusion of child star with shortstop from the San Diego Padres

CHAPTER QUIZ

1. How many times does Jonathan Franzen claim he ate out in 1999, the year he turned 40?
a. Zero (0)
b. One (1)
c. Fifteen (15)
d. Fifty-nine (59)

2. TRUE OR FALSE?
During the writing of this introduction, one author uttered the phrase "Woot! Woot! Break it down! Bagel time!"

3. ESSAY QUESTION
Write the Great American Novel.

Turned 40: 7/2/1987
Profession: Malcontent
Alter ego: Costanza
Status of enthusiasm: Curbed
Car: Prius

LARRY DAVID
MADE SOMETHING OUT OF NOTHING

"My standard response when people would ask me 'What are you gonna do when you get out [of college]?' was 'Ah, somethin'll turn up.'"

—*David, to* The New Yorker

BUILDUP: After floundering as a bra salesman, a cabbie, and a paralegal, Larry David took up comedy in his late 20s. He spent the next 10 years just barely scraping by on the laugh circuit, alternately killing and storming off stage.

BREAKTHROUGH: With nothing to lose, the 41-year-old David and his old pal Jerry Seinfeld pitched NBC a sitcom about nothing. The network was skeptical, especially of David, who would serve as head writer and producer. Still, they agreed to a pilot. Nine seasons, and more than $400 million later, they had the last laugh.

YOU STILL HAVE TIME TO
WRITE A HIT SITCOM

1. Meet an immensely popular fellow comedian; strike up first of many weird conversations about weird stuff, like "those fig bars in cellophane, without a label, that look like somebody made them in their basement?" **1 HOUR**

2. Continue on standup comedy circuit; one night, just for kicks, take the stage, check out the room, say, "Never mind," and leave. **7 YEARS**

3. Join writing crew of *Saturday Night Live*; get one sketch aired during entire season of employment. **1 YEAR**

4. Return to standup comedy, struggle to pay rent. **3 YEARS**

5. Develop sitcom pilot with the immensely popular fellow comedian, who has by now been discovered by network executives. **1 YEAR**

Age at completion
54 YEARS, 1 HOUR

Turned 40: 6/14/1971
Profession: Maid
Residence: Dee-luxe apartment
Anagram: A Grabs Limb
Alternate residence: 227

MARLA GIBBS
MOVED ON UP

BUILDUP: Marla Gibbs, who married at age 13 and had three kids by 20, hadn't landed a single acting gig by age 40. She had, however, worked as a receptionist, switchboard operator, and reservations clerk for United Airlines.

BREAKTHROUGH: After taking a couple of acting classes, 44-year-old Gibbs auditioned for a guest spot as the wisecracking maid Florence on a new TV show called *The Jeffersons*. She got the part. After the show became a hit, Gibbs quit her day job at United to concentrate on dishing out wisecracks.

Turned 40: 610 AD
Profession: Prophet
Breakthrough work: *Koran*
Favorite vacation spot: Mecca
Pet peeve: Roaming charges (unconfirmed)

MUHAMMAD
MOVED ON WAY UP

BUILDUP: After marrying a rich widower at age 25, the future prophet couldn't muster much enthusiasm for the merchant business.

BREAKTHROUGH: Alone on a retreat to Mount Hira at age 40, he received his first divine communication. The Archangel Gabriel appeared, commanding Muhammad to preach the "one true religion" he would later set down in the *Koran*. In the three years following his first revelation, only 40 people accepted the new faith. Nearly fourteen hundred years later, that number was one billion.

LIFE BEGINS AT 40

Small town news-paper editor Kennesaw H. Clark (Will Rogers) goes up against the town banker and local political boss (George Barbier) in defense of a young man recently released from jail. (1935, Fox Film Corporation)

Turned 40: 10/4/1986
Profession: Actressivist
Upbringing: Conservative Catholic
Bad pun regarding 12-years-her-junior partner: "Are you Robbins the cradle?"
Brochure modeling credits: Watergate Hotel

SUSAN SARANDON

CUT THE BULL

"Sexuality... is something that develops and becomes stronger and stronger the older you get... If you can continue to say yes to life and to maintain a certain generosity of spirit, you become more and more of who you are."

—*Sarandon, on sexuality after 40*

BUILDUP: By 40, Sarandon had inspired more midnight screenings and popcorn tossing than any actress of her generation. Unfortunately, *The Rocky Horror Picture Show* had not ignited Sarandon's career as a sexy leading lady.

BREAKTHROUGH: Sarandon finally became a bona fide star and sex symbol for the middle-aged with her performance in *Bull Durham* at age 42, and cemented that status with *Thelma & Louise* at 45. In her 40s, she was nominated for four Oscars, of which she won one.

Turned 40: 8/6/1951
Profession: First Lady of television comedy
On to-do list: Some 'splaining
Advice about aging: "The secret of staying young is to live honestly, eat slowly, and lie about your age."

LUCILLE BALL

FOUND LOVE

BUILDUP: Lucille Ball made it onto the big screen at 22, playing roles as varied as "girl," "flower girl," and "chorus girl." In her 30s, she landed enough star roles in questionable films to earn the nickname "Queen of the B Movies."

BREAKTHROUGH: Lucy's career didn't take off until she and husband Desi Arnaz started Desilu, a company that would produce a TV series in which they would both star. *I Love Lucy* hit it big, pioneering such innovations as the three-camera technique and syndication, and Lucy rocketed to sitcom stardom.

WRITERS' BLOCKS
hitting the presses after 40

HARRIET BEECHER STOWE
Turned 40: 6/14/1851
CRIED UNCLE

Though always a literary sort, Beecher Stowe gave little indication of her talent for fiction with her first book, *Primary Geography for Children.* Then, at 40, she penned an anti-slavery masterwork. Published as a serial in an abolitionist newspaper, *Uncle Tom's Cabin* became the most important book of its era.

ROBERT LUDLUM
Turned 40: 5/25/1967
FOUND HIS IDENTITY

A prolific TV actor and stage producer, Ludlum was a "closet writer" until he busted out at 44 with *The Scarlatti Inheritance.* Over the next 30 years, he penned 20 more bestsellers and sold more than 200 million books.

MIGUEL DE CERVANTES
Turned 40: 1587
MET THE MAN OF LA MANCHA

After spending his late 20s and early 30s as a slave in Turkey, Cervantes celebrated freedom with quill and ink. His first effort, published at 41, didn't cause much stir. Later, though, he'd write *Don Quixote* from a prison in La Mancha, casting the mold for the modern novel.

KURT VONNEGUT
Turned 40: 11/11/1962

WAS BOOKING AUTOMOBILE SALES

When Vonnegut published his first novel, *Player Piano,* at age 30, critics dismissed it as "mere science fiction." He spent his 30s working at a school for disturbed students and managing a Saab dealership, among other miscellaneous pursuits, before the publication of *Cat's Cradle* a decade later brought his work to a wider audience.

JIM CRACE
Turned 40: 3/1/1986

TOLD LIES

More than a decade into a successful freelance journalism career, 40-year-old Jim Crace was offered a large advance to abandon truth for fiction. His first book, *Continent,* established his reputation as a man who wasn't afraid to make things up (like entire continents).

CAROL SHIELDS
Turned 40: 6/2/1975

GOT STONED

Shields, a mother of five, came to the conclusion that "women in fiction were either bimbos or bitches," and decided to do something about it. Her first novel, *Small Ceremonies,* hit the shelves when she turned 40. Twenty years later, she won the Pulitzer Prize for *The Stone Diaries.*

Turned 40: 12/12/1849
Profession: Honest
If he were a glass of water, he'd be: A tall glass of water
Number of They Might Be Giants albums named after him: 1
Rap name: One Cent

ABRAHAM LINCOLN
VACATED HIS OFFICE

BUILDUP: Abraham Lincoln had served one term in Congress, but his anti-Mexican War sentiment proved unpopular, and, at age 40, he failed in his bid for reelection. Frustrated, he gave up politics to practice law.

BREAKTHROUGH: Lincoln reentered politics five years later, and at 49, became a senatorial candidate for the newly formed Republican Party. Though he was eventually defeated, his debates with rival Stephen A. Douglas became the stuff of legend, and he would be elected president at age 51.

YOU STILL HAVE TIME TO
RUN FOR OFFICE

1 Learn the nuances of local political landscape, especially garbage and education. **1 YEAR**

2 Declare candidacy for councilman. Say, "I will CLEAN UP garbage and RAISE test scores." **1 DAY**

3 Establish team of castoffs and senior citizens to staff headquarters (your garage). **3 MONTHS**

4 Knock on every door in town. Say, "Hi, I'm your neighbor and I'm running for town council." Learn to step back quickly when doors slam in your face. Collect enough signatures to get on ballot. **6 MONTHS**

5 Cross fingers as town's 63 interested voters rush to polls to choose between you and a 19-year-old college kid. **1 DAY**

Age at completion
41 YEARS, 9 MONTHS, 2 DAYS

Turned 40: 8/17/1999
Profession: Great American novelist
Draft pages of *The Corrections* discarded: 1,000+
Number of Oprah's Book Club books: 1 (rescinded)
Favorite section of newspaper: The Corrections

JONATHAN FRANZEN
ATE RAMEN

"If you watch an office building getting constructed, workers spend nearly a year digging around in the dirt, and then the thing goes up in about two weeks. It's just like that."

—*Franzen, on writing a novel*

BUILDUP: As 40 dawned, things looked bleak for Jonathan Franzen. He had split from his wife, his first two books were commercial duds, and he was holed up alone trying to finish a book he'd been working on for five years.

BREAKTHROUGH: After trashing all but one chapter of his unfinished work, 41-year-old Franzen finally got rolling, cranking out over 400 pages of prose in about 10 months. When published the following year, *The Corrections* was hailed as a work of genius, netting the scribe fame, fortune—and even Oprah's wrath.

Turned 40: 2/3/1947
Profession: Sailor
Drink: Bloody Mary
Side project: Unsuccessful congressional bid
Favorite section of newspaper: Travel

JAMES MICHENER
WAS YOUNGER THAN SPRINGTIME

BUILDUP: With World War II calling from across the globe, a young James Michener joined the Navy, where he soaked up the people and the islands of the South Pacific.

BREAKTHROUGH: At 40, Michener turned his wartime observations into his first book, *Tales of the South Pacific,* which he anonymously sent to his old publishing employer. The next year it won the Pulitzer Prize. Forty more books followed, though only the first had the depth of plot necessary to become a Broadway musical.

Turned 40: 10/2/1955
Profession: Frying pan purveyor
Number of Williams-Sonoma stores in North America: 239
Duraclear margarita glasses: $44 (plus shipping and handling)
Bane of existence: Spork (unconfirmed)

CHUCK WILLIAMS
SET UP SHOP IN SONOMA

BUILDUP: On vacation from his job as a building contractor in the northern California town of Sonoma, Chuck Williams traveled to Paris. There, the 38-year-old became transfixed with high-end kitchenware unavailable in the U.S.

BREAKTHROUGH: At age 41, Williams opened the doors of the first Williams-Sonoma store. Wealthy San Franciscans vacationing in Sonoma fell in love with its assortment of copper pots, sauté pans, lemon zesters, and the like. Two years later, Williams moved his shop into the city, planting the seed for a national chain.

Turned 40: 7/7/1946*
Profession: Hurler
Best Pitch: Bat Dodget
*Paige's age is a mystery; he once said, "Age is a question of mind over matter. If you don't mind, it doesn't matter."

SATCHEL PAIGE
WAS PROMOTED TO MAJOR

BUILDUP: For more than 20 years, Paige dominated the Negro Leagues with a devastating fastball and flair to match. He claims to have won 104 of 105 games in one year alone.

BREAKTHROUGH: A year after Jackie Robinson broke the color barrier in Major League Baseball, the Cleveland Indians called on Paige to join the team in the middle of a pennant race. At 42, Paige became the oldest rookie in major league history. The Indians won the pennant, and Paige went on to win 28 games in his major league career.

RUN A SUCCESSFUL SPORTS TEAM

1 Find enormous financial success running your own business (ideally inherited from parents). Sell or take business public, making you "liquid." Roll around naked in money. Get bored. **10 YEARS**

2 Assemble group of fellow investors with an eye towards buying a sports team, ensuring you keep the majority position. **1 MONTH**

3 Practice recitation of pompous quotes about winning ("Winning is the most important thing in my life, after breathing. Breathing first, winning next"). **1 YEAR**

4 Submit to bidding process for team. Write large number on the piece of paper your investment bankers will seal in an envelope and pass along to the league office. **6 MONTHS**

5 Awake as high bidder. Prepare to spend rest of lifetime uttering pompous quotes about winning. **1 DAY**

Age at which you're in the owner's box

50 YEARS, 7 MONTHS, 2 WEEKS, & A DAY

Turned 40: 7/4/1970
Profession: Evil Emperor
Nickname: The Cleveland Steamer
Favorite month: October
Favorite legume: Peanuts

GEORGE STEINBRENNER
WAS NOT YET THE BOSS

BUILDUP: After trying his hand at coaching football and basketball in his 20s, George Steinbrenner returned to helm his family's business, a Great Lakes shipping company.

BREAKTHROUGH: Refusing to let his sporting dreams die, the 41-year-old Steinbrenner offered $9 million for the Cleveland Indians. Rebuffed, he assembled a group of investors to purchase the New York Yankees for $10 million. Over the next 30 years, he'd change managers 20 times, but also win six World Series, making the Bombers America's most valuable franchise.

CHAPTER 3

"Ho, pretty page, with the dimpled chin
That never has known thé barber's shear,
All your wish is woman to win,
This is the way that boys begin.
Wait till you come to Forty Year."

—*Thackeray*

LOVE, SEX & FAMILY AT 40

A ccording to Dr. Joyce Brothers, differences between men and women "reach an all-time high at about age 40." Other esteemed psychiatry texts have noted that "sometimes, about age 40, 'sexual burnout' occurs." Well, our research suggests that this is far from the norm.

Quite the contrary, 40somethings are having sex 1.8 times a week. That's almost 100 times a year, which, when you think about it, is pretty darn sexy.

Other 40somethings have managed to put aside their "differences" long enough to make a baby, or to adopt, or to find a third spouse. See, the thing about love and sex—even parenthood—is that even if you're old and decrepit, you can still enjoy it.

MOST SHOCKING REVELATION

Someone in this chapter has been married more times than Elizabeth Taylor. (p. 64)

LEAST SHOCKING REVELATION

40-year-old Michael Jackson had marriage woes. (p. 65)

THE FUNNIEST JOKE WE HEARD THIS WEEK

Why do melons get married? Cantaloupe!

OMITTED DATA

Data: Scientists who remain unmarried reach their productivity peak at 40, much later than wedded scientists
Reason Omitted: Scientists do it in a test tube

Data: Median Age of Second Divorce: Men 39.3, Women 37
Reason Omitted: Still in litigation

Data: Orgasm statistics such as, 78% of men and 33% of women ages 40–44 always had an orgasm with their partner
Reason Omitted: Faked

Data: Virgins at age 40
Reason Omitted: So depressing

CHAPTER QUIZ

1. Which one of the following baby names was chosen for "environmental implications"?
a. Rocco
b. Lourdes
c. Gaia
d. Alizeh Keshvar

2. TRUE OR FALSE?
Stella got her groove back.

3. ESSAY QUESTION
Kinsey observed, "Considering the physiology of sexual response and the mammalian backgrounds of human behavior, it is not so difficult to explain why a human animal does a particular thing sexually. It is more difficult to explain why each and every individual is not involved in every type of sexual activity." What's *your* excuse?

HITCHED? · · · · · · · · · · **91%** **HAVE BEEN MARRIED** · · · · · · · · ·
women in their 40s

66% married once

· · **49%** still married

21% married twice

· · **16%** still married

5% married three or more times

· · **3%** still married

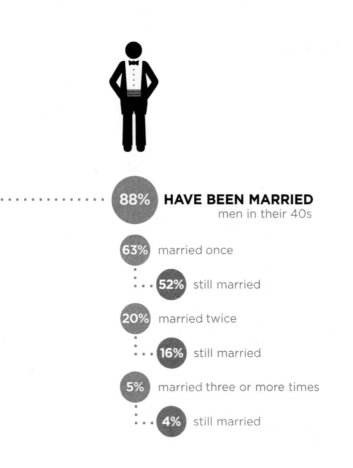

88% **HAVE BEEN MARRIED**
men in their 40s

63% married once

52% still married

20% married twice

16% still married

5% married three or more times

4% still married

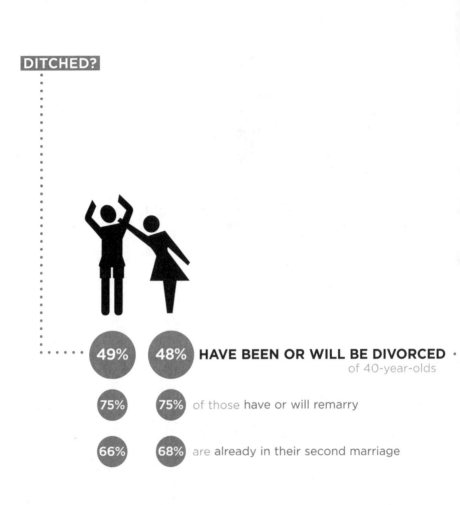

49% **48%** **HAVE BEEN OR WILL BE DIVORCED**
of 40-year-olds

75% **75%** of those have or will remarry

66% **68%** are already in their second marriage

FROM SEA TO SHINING SEE YOU LATER
marriage and divorce rates by region

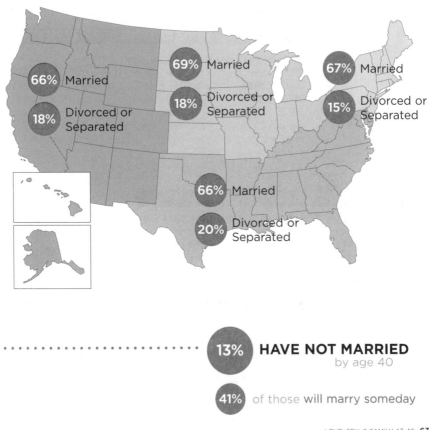

66% Married

18% Divorced or Separated

69% Married

18% Divorced or Separated

67% Married

15% Divorced or Separated

66% Married

20% Divorced or Separated

13% **HAVE NOT MARRIED**
by age 40

41% of those will marry someday

ALTARED STATES
engaged, married, or divorced at 40

LIZ TAYLOR
Turned 40: 2/27/1962

WAS ON HUSBAND NUMBER FIVE

The Hollywood star, wed for the first time at 18, was on her fifth husband, actor Richard Burton. They'd met on the set of *Cleopatra* soon after Taylor turned 30. Eight years after their nuptials, the duo starred in the first-ever made-for-TV movie, *Divorce His, Divorce Hers,* and promptly did exactly that. Two years later, they remarried—for all of 10 months. For Taylor, two additional husbands lay ahead.

DEZERRIE CORTES
Turned 40: 2003

TIED HER 27TH KNOT

The most accomplished in a long line of New York City "turbo-brides," Cortes got hitched for the 27th time at age 40. The problem? The marriages were all shams. When found out, Cortes was sentenced to six months in jail.

GEORGE CLOONEY
Turned 40: 5/6/2001

WAS SINGLE AND HANDSOME

Hollywood's most eligible bachelor proved that the Sexiest Man Alive didn't need a bride to find satisfaction. After hitting age 40 without a steady partner by his side, Clooney confided to *Vanity Fair* that he still enjoyed the life of the single man. "Here's the great thing about dating," he said. "You get to start over and go, 'I'm a really nice guy.' And by virtue of saying it, you can be it."

MICHAEL JACKSON
Turned 40: 8/29/1998
GOT HIS DUCKS IN A ROWE

Following the demise of his marriage with Lisa Marie Presley, Jacko found fresh love. He tied the knot (in a secretive ceremony) with nurse Debbie Rowe at age 38. The marriage lasted three years but produced two kids, Paris and Prince Michael. When they divorced two years later, Rowe surrendered custody rights to the children, reputedly for a $30 million payoff from Jackson.

CANDACE BUSHNELL
Turned 40: 12/1/1998
GOT CARRIED AWAY AT LAST

Like her alter ego, Carrie Bradshaw, *Sex and the City* author Bushnell mowed through a long lineup of suitors in her 30s. Still single at 43, she attended a benefit party for the New York City Ballet and hit it off with one of the dancers, Charles Askegard. Eight weeks later, the two were married on a beach in Nantucket. At the time of the wedding, one of Bushnell's friends noted, "It's the end of an era, definitely."

BABY ON BOARD / 82% **HAVE GIVEN BIRTH**
by their early 40s

 17% one child born

 35% two children born

 19% three children born

11% four or more children born

"The children despise their parents until the age of 40, when they suddenly become just like them—thus preserving the system."

—Quentin Crewe

·············· **ALL IN THE FAMILY**

8% live with a child of a relative, friend, or partner of women in their early 40s

6% live with a stepchild

2% live with an adopted child

1% are looking to adopt

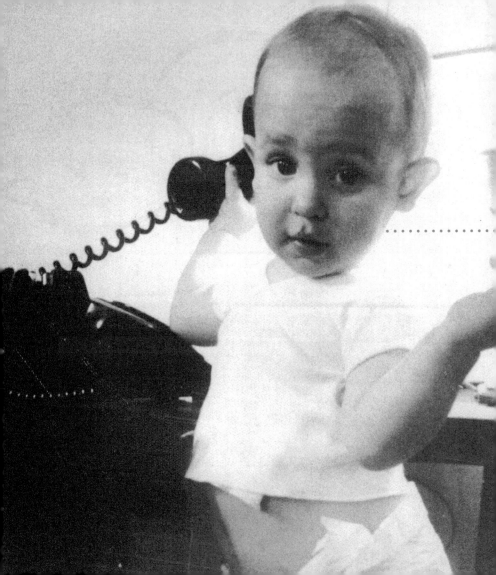

The American College of Obstetricians and Gynecologists' report says that with the current interest in health and fitness, "many women may find themselves in better shape than they were at a younger age." Similarly, there is no precise age that is considered "an unsafe turning point" for women wanting to be pregnant.

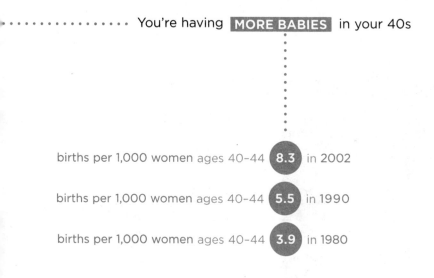

You're having **MORE BABIES** in your 40s

births per 1,000 women ages 40–44 **8.3** in 2002

births per 1,000 women ages 40–44 **5.5** in 1990

births per 1,000 women ages 40–44 **3.9** in 1980

OH, LOURDES!

celebrities pregnant after age 40

GEENA DAVIS
ALIZEH KESHVAR BORN 4/10/2002

Turned 40: 1/21/1996

Two months after the final airing of her eponymous and much reviled sitcom, *Geena,* Davis made her fourth trip to the altar—with a man 15 years her junior. Clearly, Davis had finally found a husband she was happy enough with to progenate, as six months later she and husband Dr. Reza Jarrahy celebrated the birth of their first child.

IMAN
ALEXANDRIA ZAHRA BORN 8/15/2000

Turned 40: 7/25/1995

Following her turn as a shape-shifting alien in *Star Trek 6,* model-turned-actress Iman married singer David Bowie. Eight years later, Iman brought two things into the world: a makeup company—and a baby daughter.

ANNETTE BENING
ELLA CORINNE BORN 4/8/2000

Turned 40: 5/29/1998

After receiving rave reviews for her performance in *American Beauty,* Bening celebrated by getting pregnant with her fourth child. She gave birth a couple of months before her 42nd birthday. At the time, husband Warren Beatty had just celebrated his 63rd birthday.

MADONNA
Turned 40: 8/16/1998

ROCCO BORN 8/1/2000

Just five days shy of her 42nd birthday, the Material Girl gave birth to her second child. Four months later, she would marry the father, Guy Ritchie. The couple would soon provide a lifetime of embarrassment for the young tyke in the form of the 2002 remake of *Swept Away*.

EMMA THOMPSON
Turned 40: 4/15/1999

JANE.COM BORN 12/4/1999

For two weeks after the birth of her baby girl, Thompson and boyfriend Greg Wise were unable to settle on a name, so in a nod to dot-com culture, they called the infant "jane.com." After the half-month deliberation, they settled on the only slightly less silly name of "Gaia." Wise explained that they chose the name because of "environmental implications."

"A 40-year-old woman is only something to men
who have loved her in her youth."

—Stendhal

men single at 40 • •

28% women single at 40

"Every man over forty is a scoundrel."

—*George Bernard Shaw*

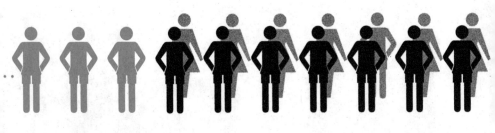

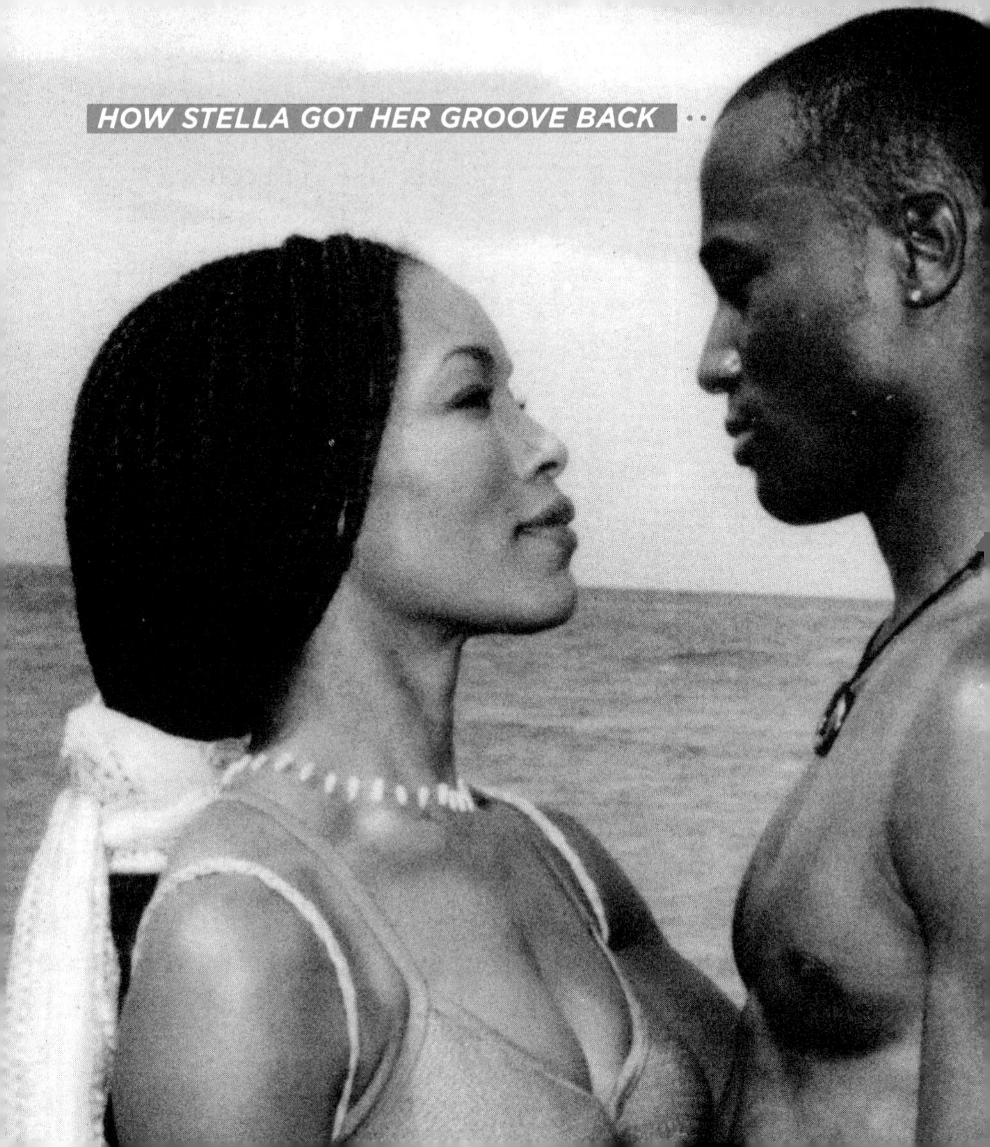

HOW STELLA GOT HER GROOVE BACK

Stella, a successful businesswoman, (**Angela Bassett**) hits her 40th birthday only to realize that she's lost her groove. What better way to get it back than a steamy affair with a man half her age (Taye Diggs)? (1998, 20th Century Fox, based on the novel by **Terry McMillan**)

Bassett was 40 when the movie hit theaters.

McMillan's breakout novel *Waiting to Exhale* was published when she was 40. She had the affair on which *Stella* was based at age 42.

Number of male
SEXUAL PARTNERS
by 40 **FOR WOMEN**

25%
1 partner

12% 2 partners

3 partners **13%**

8% 4 partners

9%
5 partners

6–9 partners **11%**

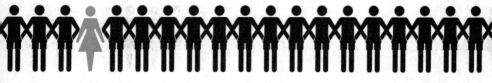

18% 10+ sexual partners

Number of female
SEXUAL PARTNERS
FOR MEN by 40

12%
1 partner

5% 2 partners

3 partners **7%**

6% 4 partners

7%
5 partners

6–9 partners **13%**

10+ sexual partners **44%**

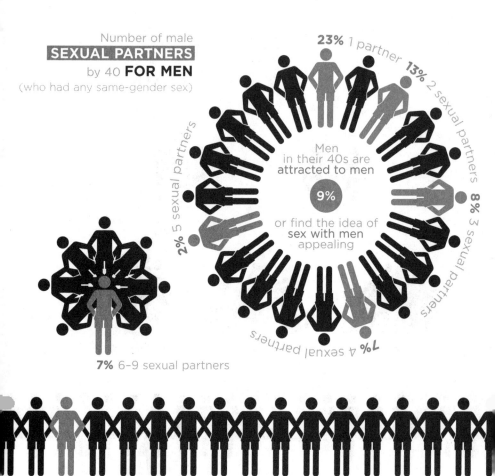

Number of male
SEXUAL PARTNERS
by 40 **FOR MEN**
(who had any same-gender sex)

23% 1 partner

13% 2 sexual partners

8% 3 sexual partners

7% 4 sexual partners

2% 5 sexual partners

Men in their 40s are **attracted to men** **9%** or find the idea of **sex with men** appealing

7% 6-9 sexual partners

41% 10+ sexual partners

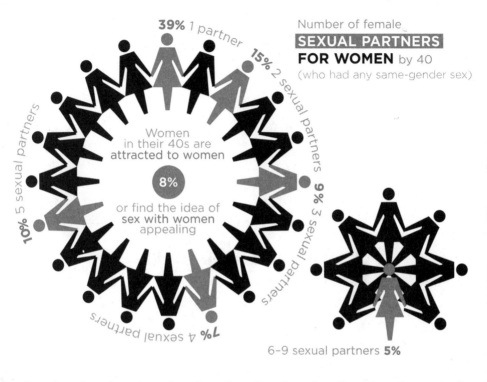

Number of female
SEXUAL PARTNERS
FOR WOMEN by 40
(who had any same-gender sex)

39% 1 partner

15% 2 sexual partners

9% 3 sexual partners

7% 4 sexual partners

10% 5 sexual partners

Women in their 40s are **attracted to women** **8%** or find the idea of **sex with women** appealing

6–9 sexual partners **5%**

10+ sexual partners **15%**

SUN	MON	TUES	
✗ 30	31	1	
6	**YOU ARE** `GETTIN' IT ON` · · · · · · · · · · · · · · 8 · · · · · ·	✗ 7	8
13	✗ 14	15	
✗ 20	21	✗ 22	

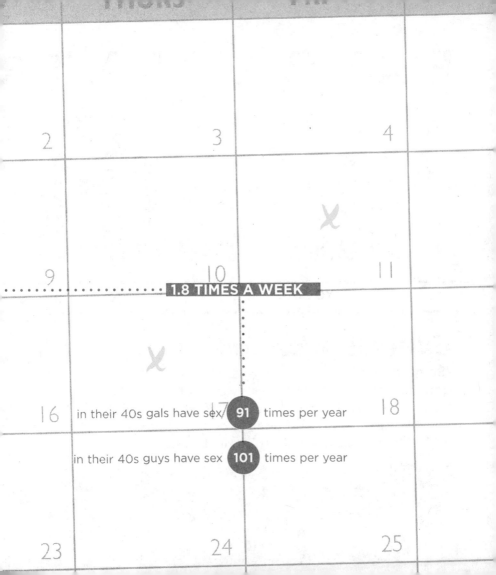

1.8 TIMES A WEEK

in their 40s gals have sex **91** times per year

in their 40s guys have sex **101** times per year

EXTRA! EXTR

MID-LIFE

WELCOME TO THE

Experts Wonder... Is It Real?

"Some psychology experts don't acknowledge the existence of a 'midlife crisis.' They suggest at around age 40 we become aware of an unidentifiable gnawing concern or dissatisfaction with the way things are...but no crisis," writes The Cato Institute.

! EXTRA!

WEATHER:
GLOOMY

CRISIS!

NEXT TWENTY YEARS!

AGE 40

OH, IT'S REAL!

Reports *The Wall Street Journal,* "The midlife crisis is a cliche—until you have one. **One-fourth of Americans age 40 through 53 say they've had a midlife crisis,** usually between their late 30s and early 50s, says a study of 724 adults by Elaine Wethington, a Cornell University professor."

THE SHOCKING CONSEQUENCES!

Ann-Margret shuns husband Bruce Dern when she discovers his attention has turned toward young girls and adult toys in the romantic comedy *Middle Age Crazy* (1980, 20th Century Fox).

ADVICE CORNER: ASK CARL!
STAYING JUNG WITH PSYCHOLOGY

Dear Carl,
I just hit 40 this morning, and I'm feeling kind of bummed! Also, slightly less principled! My wine seems kind of turgid, too. Am I the only one? Or are there others out there just like me?

Sincerely, Mid-Life Chris

Dear MLC,
Statistical tables show a rise in the frequency of cases of mental depression in men about 40. In women the neurotic difficulties generally begin somewhat earlier. We see that in this phase of life—between 35 and 40—a significant change in the human psyche is in preparation....

It also frequently happens that the convictions and principles which have hitherto been accepted—especially in moral principles—commence to harden and to grow increasingly rigid...The wine of youth does not always clear with advancing years; oftentimes it grows turgid...The very frequent neurotic disturbances of adult years have this in common, that they betray the attempt to carry the psychic dispositions of youth beyond the threshold of the so-called years of discretion....

At the stroke of noon the descent begins. And the descent means the reversal of all the ideas and values that we cherished in the morning....

Wholly unprepared, they embark upon the second half of life. Or are there perhaps colleges for 40-year-olds which prepare them for their coming life and its demands as the ordinary colleges introduce our young people to a knowledge of the world of life? No, there are none.

Yours, Carl Jung

Noted pyschologist Carl Jung's latest work is Modern Man In Search of a Soul *(1933), from which the above is excerpted.*

THE BAD NEWS!

Gail Sheehy, in her 1976 book *Passages*, spells out in painful detail what you have to fear from middle age: "The loss of youth, the faltering of physical powers we have always taken for granted, the fading purpose of stereotyped roles by which we have thus far identified ourselves, the spiritual dilemma of having no absolute answers—any or all of these shocks can give this passage the character of crisis. Such thoughts usher in a decade between 35 and 45 that can be called the Deadline Decade. It is a time of both danger and opportunity...Whatever rung of achievement he has reached, the man of 40 usually feels stale, restless, burdened, and unappreciated."

THE GOOD NEWS

When asked, "If you could stop time and live forever in good health at a particular age, what age would you like to live at?" Americans chose 41, making it the nation's "ideal age." 40somethings consider their "ideal age" to be 40. A paltry 2% of all respondents said they would pick an age between 18 and 24.

EVERYONE'S GOT AN OPINION!

Victoria Secunda noted, "Middle age is a period when a man, for the first time, may be plumbing his 'feminine' side—the part that cries easily at movies, that needs to hold tenderly and to be held by the people he most loves, the part that is aware of his emotional losses." **Mason Cooley** complained, "Middle age went by while I was mourning for my lost youth." **Ronald Reagan** observed, "Middle age is when you're faced with two temptations and you choose the one that will get you home by 9 o'clock." **J. Bailey Molineux** stated, "One of the advantages of the midlife crisis is that it can enable a man to break out from under the prohibitions of the masculine mystique that demands so much of him and develop the other, previously ignored half of himself; age 40, he should have put away childish things and not have to prove his manliness any more."

"Young fellows are tempted by girls, men who are 30 years old are tempted by gold, when they are 40 years old they are tempted by honor and glory."

—Martin Luther

MONEY & POWER AT 40

Not everybody is rich and powerful by 40, but in one way or another, we're all sought after. As your collection agent notes, "Dear Friend, this claim has been turned over to our office for collection. I want to let you know that we intend to pursue this claim and reserve the right to report this matter to the credit bureau, as well as pursue other remedies. Should it be economically feasible, that would include litigation. I fully realize that you may contest the merits of this claim. Certainly, it is not my intent to threaten or alarm you about this matter. I would hope that you take a moment and seriously consider the consequences of your actions. Contacting our office to remedy the situation may prove to be a wise move."

MOST SHOCKING REVELATION
Henry Ford was rumored to have been a terrible driver—always tailgated, never put on his blinker, etc. (p. 94)

LEAST SHOCKING REVELATION
When he was 40, Ronald Reagan shared billing with a chimp. (p. 110)

CHAPTER-TITLE TRANSLATIONS
dinero y energía
geld und energie
argent et puissance
soldi ed alimentazione
dinheiro e poder
(*Note:* Google's translation engine may have misinterpreted the word "power.")

OMITTED DATA

Data: In 2002, the U.S. Army increased the maximum age for drill sergeants to 40
Reason Omitted: Ten-hut!

Data: "The counselor at law who, perhaps, at near forty years of age, begins to make something by his profession, ought to receive the retribution, not only of his own so tedious and expensive education, but of that of more than twenty others who are never likely to make any thing by it." –Adam Smith, *Wealth of Nations*
Reason Omitted: Huh? Oh, sorry, did I doze off?

CHAPTER QUIZ

1. What is "Bush Exploration?"
a. A failed oil company
b. A fraternity prank
c. A safari adventure
d. A gynecological procedure

2. TRUE OR FALSE?
Genghis Khan was actually a pretty nice guy, once you got to know him.

3. ESSAY QUESTION:
When you were 11 years old, you wanted to be a professional athlete, a ballerina, or an astronaut. You are none of those things. Explain where you went wrong.

ALTERNATE QUESTION:
You are a professional athlete, a ballerina, or an astronaut. Nice work! Proceed to the next chapter.

HEADING FOR THE CORNER OFFICE?

40-year-olds have **4.6 YEARS** median time at current job

18% under 1 year

31% 1-4 years

21% 5-9 years

24% 10-19 years

6% 20+ years

34% of CEOs are in their 40s

31% of Lawyers

32% of Physicians & Surgeons

27% of Computer Programmers

.... **40SOMETHINGS MAKE UP** **26%** **OF THE WORKFORCE**

27% of Artists

19% of Actors

11% of Waiters & Waitresses

25% of Funeral Directors

Turned 40: 7/30/1903
Profession: Mechanic
Favorite gear: Third (unconfirmed)

HENRY FORD
STARTED HIS ENGINE

AT 40: Fresh off two failed attempts to launch an automobile manufacturing company, Ford finally found the road to success with the Ford Motor Company. In the early days, with Henry himself serving as chief engineer, the company churned out a couple of cars a day. It was not until a decade later that Ford would hit upon the idea of the continuous, moving assembly line to produce his beloved Model T. The innovation made cars affordable for most Americans. Soon, traffic came to a grinding halt from sea to shining sea.

"Anyone who stops learning is old, whether at 20 or 80. Anyone who keeps learning stays young. The greatest thing in life is to keep your mind young."

—Ford

86% **OWN A CAR**
of families
headed by 35-44

AVERAGE VALUE · $12,400

THE BUCK STARTS HERE...

 8% of teens think they'll be worth more than $1 million at 40

 4% think they'll be worth $500,000–$1 million

 30% think they'll be worth $100,000–$500,000

 57% think they'll be worth $25,000–$100,000

 1% think they'll be worth less than $25,000

...AND STOPS HERE $259,500

actual mean net worth for families headed by people 35-44

WORN OUT? <mark>62 YEARS</mark> **AVERAGE EXPECTED RETIREMENT AGE**

for people in their 40s

 HAVE SET UP RETIREMENT ACCOUNTS · · · ·

of families headed by people 35-44

· median value **$28,500**

23% own savings bonds · · · · · median value **$1,000**

22% own stocks · · · · · · · · · · median value **$15,000**

27% own life insurance · · · · · · median value **$5,300**

18% own mutual funds · · · · · median value **$17,500**

Turned 40: 3/29/1958
Profession: Bargain billionaire
Arch enemies: Mom and Pop

SAM WALTON

PRICE GOUGED

AT 40: Like most other retailers in the late 1950s, Walton was marking up prices left and right. But as he looked to expand his retail operation, Walton saw the discount writing on the wall. At 44, he abandoned his price-gouging ways and opened the first Wal-Mart

..WMT 50 1/2 UP 1/2...MSO 11 1/16 DN 1/

in Rogers, AR. The store marked the beginning of the golden age of low-low prices. By age 67, Walton was the richest man in America, peddling everything from inexpensive jeans to off-price milk to Wal-Mart–approved sanitized music—non-explicit lyrics guaranteed!

Turned 40: 2/14/1982
Profession: Mayor, NYC
Previous profession: Player, NYC

MICHAEL BLOOMBERG
RAN WITH THE BULLS

AT 40: A year after he was unceremoniously fired from a high-level finance job at Salomon Brothers, Bloomberg was muscling his way back onto Wall Street. Flush with capital from his Salomon severance package, he started the financial information company Bloomberg L.P.

TWX 16 1/8 DN 3/8...PXR 65 8/16 UP 11/1

He promptly sold 20 subscriptions to Merrill Lynch. More subscriptions, a news organization, and radio and television programming followed. Twenty years and several billion dollars later, Bloomberg gave up the helm of his own ship to pilot New York City.

Reginald Istrant
190 Barhour Street
Providence, R.I. 02910

Dear Mr. Istrant,

This claim has been _____ ___ __ ___ office for collection. I want to let you know that you Hide/Seek C____ Credit Bureau, as well as pursue other remedies. Should it be economically agency intends to pursue this claim and reserve the right to report this _____ that would include litigation.

___ process of litigation has not yet been instituted. If it happens, it will be pursued thr local attorney __ ____ ___ with state statutes. Should a Judgment be issued against result of this proce__ ___ ___ ___ be charged with court costs, and, in some case fees. After a Judgment is issued a _____ ___editor has a number of methods available to Judgment.

It might be valuable for you to check the laws ___ your State pertaining to the s

DROWNING? **88%** **CARRY DEBT** ·
of families headed by people 35–44

I fully realize that you may contest the merits of this claim. Certainly, it threaten or alarm you about this matter. I would hope that you take a consider the consequences of your actions.

Contacting our office to remedy the situation may prove to be

• median balance **$60,600**

54% have a credit-card balance • • • median balance **$2,000**

57% have an installment loan • • • • • median balance **$11,100**

60% have a mortgage • • • • • • • • • • median balance **$80,000**

YOU CAN'T USE YOUR DAMN COMPUTER · · · · · · · · ·

40somethings make up 23% of Internet users but only

 20% of the U.S. population

"If you're part of the Baby Boom generation, there are probably days when you find yourself wondering what's gone wrong with your personal computer. Suddenly, text on the screen is harder to read, email alerts and other sounds are harder to hear, and the keyboard seems to have taken on a life of its own—making all sorts of mistakes.

"If you're over age 40, there's a good chance your computer isn't the problem. Instead, you may be entering the 'awkward age of computing,' when age-related changes in vision, hearing, and dexterity require most of us to make a few adjustments to our PCs."

—"Overview of Aging and Accessible Technology"
Microsoft Corp.

 23% of middle aged Americans suspect they have been subjected to age-related employment discrimination since turning 40.

LEVER 2000? 62% **ARE REGISTERED TO VOTE** at 40

64% of women

62% of men

53% **ACTUALLY VOTED** in the 2000 presidential election

"At 20 years of age, the will reigns; at 30, the wit; and at 40, the judgment." • • • • • • • • • • • • • • • • • • •
—*Ben Franklin*

Teddy Roosevelt age 42

John F. Kennedy age 43

Bill Clinton age 46

Ulysses S. Grant age 46

 Grover Cleveland age 47

Franklin Pierce age 48

YOUNG GUNS

U.S. Presidents who took office in their 40s

 James K. Polk age 49

 James Garfield age 49

Turned 40: 12/11/1983
Profession: Presidential hopeful, 2004
Favorite food: Chocolate chip cookies

JOHN KERRY
TOOK THE FLOOR

AT 40: As a newly minted senator from Massachusetts, 40-year-old Kerry was busy crafting opinions on both sides of many of the important issues of the day. At 44, he formed the Kerry Committee to investigate the use of money earmarked for counter-narcotic operations to fund Nicaraguan contras, which led to the Oliver North hearings. He continued to serve through 2004, when at age 60 he became the Democratic nominee for President. And handsome!

Turned 40: 7/6/1986
Profession: 43rd president
Office pets: Spot (dog), Barney (dog), India (cat), Ofelia (longhorn)

GEORGE W. BUSH
DIDN'T HIT A GUSHER

AT 40: Bush gave up alcohol, though the benefits were not immediately apparent. He was in the middle of a spectacular string of oil company failures. After the third oil company he was involved with ended up in the red, 42-year-old Bush figured the well was finally dry and cashed in his stock to buy a share in the Texas Rangers, becoming a managing partner. Six years later, Texas elected Bush its governor, launching him on a political trajectory that would carry him to the Oval Office at age 54.

STARS EARN THEIR STRIPES
future U.S. Presidents at 40

RONALD REAGAN
Turned 40: 2/6/1951
WAS MONKEYING AROUND

A B-list actor at 40, Reagan starred alongside a chimpanzee in the romance comedy *Bedtime for Bonzo* (yes, there was a woman involved too). A year later, Reagan got serious, just saying yes to marrying his future First Lady Nancy Davis.

GEORGE WASHINGTON
Turned 40: 2/22/1772
HAD SOME REVOLUTIONARY IDEAS

Tired of Great Britain's colonial policies, Washington was fomenting revolution. When he was 43, the Second Continental Congress unanimously voted Washington to be commander and chief of the colonial troops.

JOHN F. KENNEDY
Turned 40: 5/29/1957
MUGGED FOR THE CAMERA

Happy birthday, Mr. President! At 40, Kennedy bided his time in the Senate. Three years later, in the first televised presidential debates, the telegenic Kennedy defeated a profusely sweating Nixon. He remains the youngest elected president in U.S. history.

RICHARD NIXON
Turned 40: 1/9/1953

PLAYED CHECKERS

Two years into his first Senate term, Nixon was tapped by Eisenhower to run for vice president. He did much of the campaign's dirty work, and it came back to bite him when he was accused of receiving gifts from wealthy supporters. His famous "Checkers speech" saved the day—and the dog. His dog (a campaign gift that Nixon refused to return) lapped it up, and so did the country. By 40, he was Ike's right-hand man.

THEODORE ROOSEVELT
Turned 40: 10/27/1898

FLASHED HIS BIG STICK

At age 42, six months after his election as vice president, Roosevelt became the youngest Commander-in-Chief in U.S. history when he assumed the office after President McKinley was assassinated.

GANDHI
WAS GETTING CIVIL

AT 40: Mahatma Gandhi was making a comfortable living practicing law in South Africa, his home since age 24. His political awakening was already under way; four years earlier, dismayed by the treatment Indians received in South Africa, he launched his first civil disobedience campaign. A month after turning 40, he authored a short treatise, "Indian Home Rule," outlining his thoughts on the principles of nonviolence. He'd return to India at age 46 and commence a movement for independence that reached its goal in 1947, when Gandhi was 77.

Turned 40: circa 1202 AD
Profession: Bleeder
Meaning of "Genghis Khan": "Universal Ruler"

GENGHIS KHAN
WASN'T

AT 40: The young Khan was still fighting for supremacy over his people, to say nothing of the rest of the world. Having waged a decade's worth of war in his attempt to unify Mongolia, young Genghis's reputation as a leader was on the rise. At age 44, after a series of key victories, he was acknowledged as leader and given the title Genghis Khan. In the next 20 years, he'd lay waste to most of Asia, ruling an empire that stretched from the Caspian Sea to Beijing.

THEY SHOOK UP THE WORLD

international leaders at 40

MARGARET THATCHER Turned 40: 10/13/1965
WAS NOT YET A MILK SNATCHER

Thatcher had established herself as a member of British Parliament at 40 and was busy working her way up the conservative party ladder in a time honored way: by accusing her opponents of being "communists." She did not become "Thatcher, Milk Snatcher" until age 46, when she ended the U.K. free-milk school program.

MAO TSE-TUNG Turned 40: 12/26/1933
TOOK A HIKE

Having sought refuge in the mountains of southeast China at age 38, Mao was holed up there with his ragtag band of fellow revolutionaries when he turned 40. There, he fleshed out his communist doctrines and built the Red Army that would seize power in China when Mao was 55.

NAPOLEON Turned 40: 8/15/1809
WAS NURSING A COMPLEX

Excommunicated by the Pope two months before turning 40, Napoleon was mad as hell. Having already conquered much of Europe, the French Emperor was casting his eyes east towards Russia. Alas, a failed Russian military campaign, launched when he was 42, was the start of his downfall. At 44, Napoleon was exiled to an island off the coast of Italy.

QUEEN ISABELLA
Turned 40: 4/22/1491
SENT COLUMBUS ON HIS WAY

Having introduced the Inquisition to Spain a decade before, Queen Isabella may have been looking to better her place in the history books when, at age 40, she agreed to finance 40-year-old Christopher Columbus on a voyage across the Atlantic to Asia. Though Columbus didn't find the Far East, the deal worked out pretty well for both of them.

NELSON MANDELA
Turned 40: 7/18/1958
HAD THE TRIAL OF HIS LIFE

After over a decade spent battling apartheid in his home country of South Africa, Mandela was on trial for treason when he turned 40. Although he was acquitted three years later, he was arrested again and sentenced to jail, where he'd remain for the next three decades until his dream of a just South Africa was finally realized.

TONY BLAIR
Turned 40: 5/6/1993
LABORED FOR HIS PARTY

Having climbed the ladder of Britain's liberal Labour Party in his 20s and 30s, Blair found himself thrust into its leadership role when, at 41, the party's leader died. Blair charted a new course for the party, engineering a landslide electoral victory that made him, at age 44, the youngest British Prime Minister in two centuries.

CHAPTER 5

METER

> "The first 40 years of life give us the text;
> the next 30 supply the commentary."
> —*Arthur Schopenhauer*

 **FORTYMETER**

Think of it as the fuel gauge of life. Our patented FortyMeter device measures, by means of a complex mathematical formula, a person's accomplishments at 40 against achievements made the rest of their lives. Some of the people in this chapter were running on fumes at 40; others had just filled up at the gas station of fame...maybe for the last time.

How full is your tank? FortyMeter knows.

HOW TO READ THE FORTYMETER

Zero on the FortyMeter:
The lowest point of the person's life
in gray: what they did
in orange: when they did it

FortyArrow:
Points to FortyMeter reading at age 40
measures accomplishments at 40 in relation to High and Low
(in example, person is at 75% of maximum potential)

100 on the FortyMeter:
The person's greatest accomplishment
in gray: what they did
in orange: when they did it

The Number "40"

Found stinking drunk in a gutter
LOW: Age 67

FORTYMETER

Elected president of Harvard University
HIGH: Age 35

OMITTED DATA

Data: Steve Martin biography
Reason Omitted: Filled wild, crazy quotient with Wolfgang Puck biography

Data: Marie Curie doings at 40 (between Nobel Prizes, blah, blah, blah)
Reason Omitted: Too racy

Data: Quote from Finley Peter Dunne, "If ye live enough befure thirty, ye won't care to live at all afther fifty"
Reason Omitted: Skips forty

CHAPTER QUIZ

1. According to Billy Joel, who didn't start the fire?
a. I
b. You
c. We
d. Them

2. TRUE OR FALSE?
Johnny Depp has shared the screen with Richard Grieco *and* Andrew Dice Clay.

3. ESSAY QUESTION
Explain, in detail, the theory of General Relativity. Extra points for using the word "custard."

Turned 40: 6/9/2003
Profession: Perennially strange actor
Why he didn't get a 21 Jump Street spinoff of his own: He's no Richard Grieco.

DEPP WAS IN DEEP

AT 40: Forty was a busy age for the actor who made his name on *21 Jump Street.* As Captain Jack Sparrow in *Pirates of the Caribbean,* Depp did the impossible, proving one can make a good movie based on an amusement park ride. He continued to draw praise for his portrayal of a corrupt and eyeless CIA agent in *Once Upon a Time in Mexico,* and even managed to emerge unscathed from the lambasted *Secret Window.* All this and he still had time to serve as *People* magazine's Sexiest Man Alive.

"I'm really enjoying it. By the time you reach 40, you go, 'This isn't so bad.' Thirty was much worse."

—*Depp, to* Extra!

Costars with
Andrew Dice Clay
in teen sex romp
Private Resort
LOW: Age 22

FORTY METER

Regains pirate
ship in *The
Black Pearl*
HIGH: Age 40

Turned 40: 9/24/1976
Profession: Muppeteer
Selected Muppets voiced: Kermit the Frog, Rowlf the Dog, Dr. Teeth, Swedish Chef, Wa

HENSON GOT THINGS STARTED

AT 40: In his 30s, he'd created the puppet characters on *Sesame Street,* but Jim Henson yearned to shed the label of children's performer. A brief and unfortunate stint on *Saturday Night Live* led him to create his own comedy-variety show. When he turned 40, *The Muppet Show* was struggling through its first season on the air. But by the second season, the show began to grab fans. At its peak, *The Muppet Show* reached 235 million viewers worldwide. Pretty good for a man with his hand up a frog's ass.

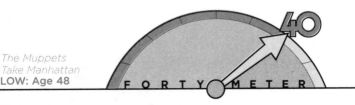

The Muppets Take Manhattan
LOW: Age 48

FORTY METER

The Muppet Movie
HIGH: Age 43

Turned 40: 11/30/1969
Profession: Muppet instigator
Partial inspiration for *Sesame Street*: *Laugh-In*

COONEY ▌ HIT THE STREET

AT 40: On the street. At age 36, while hosting a dinner party, Joan Ganz Cooney had a conversation about whether television could serve as a better educational tool for children. Intrigued, she launched a study on the issue. As a result, the Children's Television Workshop was formed, based on Cooney's vision of television that was good and good for you. A month before she turned 40, Cooney saw the foam-rubber fruits of her vision become reality with the launch of *Sesame Street*.

Catches avian pox from Big Bird (unconfirmed)
LOW: Age 47

F O R T Y   M E T E R

Date with Bert! (unconfirmed)
HIGH: Age 51

Turned 40: 6/7/1888
Profession: Synthetic symbolist
Best known for: Naked Tahitian women

GAUGUIN WAS VAN GOGHING

AT 40: The painter moved to a small town in southern France where his art dealer's cousin was setting up a painter's colony. At first, Paul Gauguin and Vincent van Gogh hit it off, living and working side by side and banging out masterpieces. But tensions mounted when winter came and the artists had to spend more time indoors. Gauguin mentioned he might like to return to Paris. Van Gogh responded by threatening Gauguin, slicing off a piece of his own ear, and delivering it to a nearby prostitute. It was at this point, for some reason, that Gauguin decided to cut short his visit.

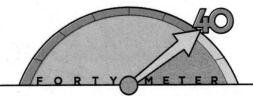

Alcohol, financial woes, and syphilis lead to suicide attempt
LOW: Age 50

FORTY METER

Travels to Tahiti, set of many of his best paintings, for first time
HIGH: Age 43

Turned 40: 8/6/1968
Profession: Pop star
Birth name: Andrew Warhola

WARHOL WASN'T DEAD YET

AT 40: Andy Warhol was still recuperating from an assassination attempt. The father of Pop Art, already famous for his Campbell's soup can prints, had been working in his studio when Valerie Solanis walked in and shot him three times in the chest. Solanis, who had acted in one of Warhol's films, was the founder and sole member of the Society for Cutting Up Men (SCUM). Warhol was mispronounced dead at the scene and would spend eight weeks in the hospital. He survived to live out his 15 minutes—give or take—of fame.

"I am a deeply superficial person."
—*Warhol*

Accepts commission from Campbell's Soup for paintings based on dry soup mixes
LOW: Age 57

Appears on episode of *The Love Boat*
HIGH: Age 57

F O R T Y M E T E R

Turned 40: 1/29/1994
Profession: Daily gabber
Actual Publication: *O: The Oprah Magazine*

OPRAH TOOK OUT THE TRASH

AT 40: Oprah Winfrey went on the offensive against sleaze. Her daily talk show, which had already won six Emmy Awards, was sliding in the ratings as racier alternatives grabbed wide-eyed viewers. Pressed to tart things up, Winfrey moved in the other direction, pledging to keep her show free of tabloid topics and, two years later, introducing Oprah's Book Club. The moves paid off: viewers eventually tired of tabloid TV and returned to Oprah's embrace.

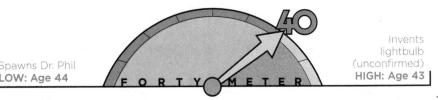

Spawns Dr. Phil
LOW: Age 44

FORTY METER

Invents
lightbulb
(unconfirmed)
HIGH: Age 43

Turned 40: 2/13/1994
Profession: Ringmaster
Actual London musical: *Jerry Springer: The Opera*

SPRINGER GOT TRASHY

AT 40: A disgraced city councilman by 31 (he paid a prostitute by personal check), Springer rebounded to become the mayor of Cincinnati at 33. Then, after a failed bid for governor, he turned to TV, becoming the anchor of a Cincinnati news station at 40. After eight years, and seven Emmys, Springer's employers asked him if he might be interested in hosting a daily talk show. Minutes later, he ditched the news and went looking for interviewees who could state with pride, "I'm pregnant by a transsexual!"

"Let's be honest. I've always said it's the stupidest show on television."
—*Springer, on* The Jerry Springer Show

Check today's local listings
LOW: Age 47+

Spearheads lowering of voting age to 18
HIGH: Age 27

Turned 40: 4/14/1919
Profession: Genius
Shampoo: Prell

EINSTEIN DEFINED GRAVITY

AT 40: Having already conquered distance and time at the tender age of 26, an older and still-wise Einstein tackled the weightiest subject of them all. At 40, he used a solar eclipse to prove that gravity pulling in one direction is equal to an acceleration in the opposite direction. It was the first major breakthrough in the study of gravity in 250 years, and it made the wild-haired scientist, who was already one of the smartest guys anybody had ever met, even more famous. Two years later, just to rub it in, he won the Nobel Prize in physics.

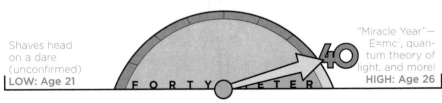

Shaves head
on a dare
(unconfirmed)
LOW: Age 21

F O R T Y   M E T E R

"Miracle Year"—
$E=mc^2$, quantum theory of
light, and more!
HIGH: Age 26

Turned 40: 7/18/1961
Profession: Some people call him a Space Cowboy
Age returned to space: 77

GLENN — DEFIED GRAVITY

> "I don't know what you could say about a day in which you've seen four beautiful sunsets."
> —*Glenn*

AT 40: John Glenn became the first American to orbit the earth. A decorated Marine pilot, and one of the original seven astronauts, Glenn circled the globe three times in the spaceship *Friendship 7*. Glenn returned a national hero, so much so that President Kennedy asked NASA not to risk his life in space again. Later in his 40s, after a bathroom accident ended his first bid for the U.S. Senate, Glenn explored a different sort of "air"-ation as an executive at Royal Crown Cola.

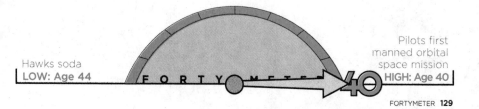

Hawks soda
LOW: Age 44

FORTYMETER

Pilots first manned orbital space mission
HIGH: Age 40

Turned 40: 11/11/2002
Profession: Perennially buff actress
Characters played named after cities: Madison, Jordan, Dallas

MOORE HAD MORE TO OFFER

AT 40: After capturing the public eye as an '80s Brat Packer, Demi Moore ascended to become the first actress ever to command an eight-figure salary—$12.5 million for baring her breasts in *Striptease*. But she all but disappeared from the screen at age 35 after the dismal showing of *G.I. Jane*. At 40, she made a comeback as a sexy ex-Angel in *Charlie's Angels: Full Throttle*. Reviewers agreed that Moore's 40-year-old physique upstaged that of her decade-younger costars. Perhaps this went to her head—soon after, she started dating a 24-year-old Ashton Kutcher.

Loses lead in *Flashdance* to Jennifer Beals
LOW: Age 20

St. Elmo's Fire
HIGH: Age 23

Turned 40: 1/10/1989
Profession: Heavy
Favorite name: George

FOREMAN WAS FIRED UP

AT 40: Ten years after he first retired from boxing, Foreman returned to the ring at age 38. By 40, he had knocked out 14 straight (carefully selected) opponents. Five years later, he beat up Michael Moorer to become the oldest heavyweight champ in history. Outside of the ring, Foreman found time to "knock the fat out of cooking." When George turned 50, Salton Inc., the maker of the George Foreman Lean Mean Grilling Machine, paid him $137.5 million for the lifetime rights to emblazon his name in kitchens across America.

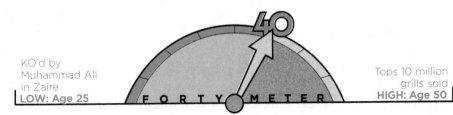

KO'd by
Muhammad Ali
in Zaire
LOW: Age 25

FORTY METER

Tops 10 million
grills sold
HIGH: Age 50

JOEL   STARTED FIRES

AT 40: No stranger to financial mismanagement (when he was 22, he unknowingly signed with a production company for life), the 40-year-old piano man fired his manager and former brother-in-law Frank Weber over "accounting irregularities." Then he sued him for $90 million. Amidst the turmoil, Billy Joel managed to produce a hit album, *Storm Front.* The album's first single was "We Didn't Start the Fire," which contained verse after verse of educational material. As for the suit, the judge awarded Joel $2 million.

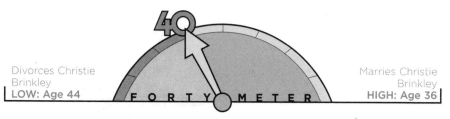

Divorces Christie
Brinkley
LOW: Age 44

Marries Christie
Brinkley
HIGH: Age 36

F O R T Y   M E T E R

Turned 40: 10/28/1954
Profession: Lab rat
Motto: Stand up straight!

SALK WAS A STANDUP GUY

AT 40: A late entrant in the race to cure polio, Jonas Salk dashed to the front of the pack in 1955 when his vaccine was proven effective. "The Man Who Saved the Children" refused to patent the vaccine, forgoing profit and endearing himself to millions worldwide who feared the disease. Still, Salk stirred the ire of his fellow scientists by failing to publicly share the credit for the vaccine. Despite his lifelong work as a polio spokesman, and his enduring philanthropy, Salk's peers never forgave him.

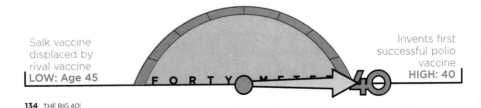

Salk vaccine displaced by rival vaccine
LOW: Age 45

Invents first successful polio vaccine
HIGH: 40

FORTY METER

Turned 40: 1/1/1775
Profession: Silversmith
Side profession: Dentist

REVERE	RODE

AT 40: Paul Revere borrowed a horse and rode from Boston to Lexington, Mass. Having seen two lanterns hanging in a church steeple—and remembering that old childhood rhyme, "One if by land, two if by sea"—he spread word of the imminent British invasion by sea that would launch the American Revolution. Though he rose to the rank of lieutenant colonel during the war, the "Midnight Ride" was the high point of Revere's military career.

"Just me and my horsy and a quart of beer/Riding across the land— kicking up sand."
—"Paul Revere," The Beastie Boys

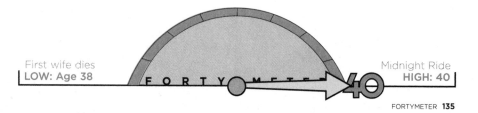

First wife dies
LOW: Age 38

Midnight Ride
HIGH: 40

FORTYMETER

Turned 40: 5/20/1986
Profession: Mooner
Will not wear: Orange

CHER WAS MOONSTRUCK

AT 40: With Sonny long behind her, Cher was in the midst of establishing herself as a box office superstar who could, when all the glitter was put aside, actually act. The trio of films released when she was 41—*Suspect, Witches of Eastwick,* and *Moonstruck*—would win her raves and, in the case of *Moonstruck,* the Oscar for Best Actress. Not content to rule the screen, Cher also breathed new life back into her singing career, hitting the charts with "I Found Someone." (She had indeed—22-year-old bagel maker Rob Camilletti.)

"Have him washed and brought to my tent."
—*Cher, on seeing Rob Camilletti for the first time, on her 40th birthday*

Dress missing one sequin (unconfirmed)
LOW: Age 28

FORTY METER

Wins Best Actress Oscar for *Moonstruck*
HIGH: Age 41

Turned 40: 4/24/1982
Profession: Crooner
Favorite color: White

STREISAND MADE YENTL SOUP

AT 40: Streisand was on the verge of fulfilling a longtime dream. Fifteen years earlier, a Hollywood newcomer, she'd read a short story titled "Yentl, The Yeshiva Boy." She vowed to make into a movie this tale of a young woman who disguises herself as a man to enter Jewish religious training. But it wasn't until just before her 40th birthday when the stars aligned. The completed film, *Yentl,* released when Streisand was 41, earned rave reviews and Babs credit as the first woman to write, direct, star in, and produce a modern feature film.

Refused extra
seat on airplane
for nose
(unconfirmed)
LOW: Age 29

FORTYMETER

Wins Best
Actress Oscar
for first
movie role,
Funny Girl
HIGH: Age 26

ROCKERS RECORDED

musicians at age 40

MICK JAGGER
Turned 40: 7/26/1983

STRUTTED BY HIMSELF

At 40, stuck in a bitter feud with Keith Richards over the direction of the Rolling Stones, Jagger recorded his first solo album, *She's the Boss.* Despite the ill will and constant threats that the band was done, a 46-year-old Jagger and 45-year-old Richards reunited for "Steel Wheels," the top-grossing tour in rock history.

TINA TURNER
Turned 40: 11/26/1978

DIDN'T LIKE IKE

Three years after walking out on Ike, Tina was struggling to stay in the spotlight. A series of mediocre solo albums didn't help her cause. But at 44, she came roaring back with *Private Dancer,* which contained three top-ten hits including "What's Love Got to Do with It."

SHERYL CROW
Turned 40: 2/11/2002

TOOK OFF THE SUN BLOCK

Stricken with a bout of writer's block in her late 30s, the former chart-topper (and onetime Michael Jackson backup singer) hadn't released a studio album in almost four years when she released *C'mon* at age 40. The album drew raves from critics and featured the summer radio smash "Soak up the Sun."

BRUCE SPRINGSTEEN
Turned 40: 9/23/1989
DID THE E STREET SHUFFLE

Sparks flew on E Street when the Boss broke up with his band at 40. Two years removed from *Tunnel of Love,* his introspective follow-up to *Born in the USA,* Springsteen decided it was time for a change. By 50, he was back on tour with his old bandmates.

BONNIE RAITT
Turned 40: 11/8/1989
LUCKED OUT

After two decades of struggle on the folk and blues club circuit, Raitt gave the music world something to talk about at age 39 with the release of her first smash-hit album, *Nick of Time.* At 40, she was in the studio recording a follow-up album, *Luck of the Draw,* that would ensconce her as a household name.

WHITNEY HOUSTON
Turned 40: 8/9/2003
CHECKED IN

Ten years after releasing the biggest single of all time ("I Will Always Love You") and 20 years after notching seven straight number one songs, Houston checked herself into rehab. It wasn't a huge surprise—a year earlier, she'd confessed to years of drug use, and four years earlier, police busted her for possession in a Hawaii airport.

Turned 40: 1/31/1987
Profession: Fast
Analgesic: Advil

RYAN | BROUGHT THE HEAT

AT 40: Nolan Ryan was still Major League Baseball's most feared fireballer. After almost 20 seasons of fastballs, the rangy Texan had enough left in the tank to lead the National League in strikeouts and ERA. In his 40s, Ryan pitched two of his seven no-hitters and won 71 games. Of course, even the Ryan Express occasionally needed a little something to dull the pain. •

"When the pitcher appears on TV in an Advil commercial and drawls, 'Ah feel ready to go another nahn innin's,' all of middle-aged America cheers him on. What man in his 40s would not like to look in the mirror and find Nolan Ryan?"

—*Time, 1990*

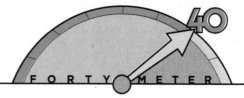

Struggles to live up to $1 million contract
LOW: Age 33

FORTY METER

Sets single-season strike-out record
HIGH: Age 26

Turned 40: 7/8/1989
Profession: Celebrity chef
Number of Las Vegas restaurants: 3

PUCK SHOT, SCORED

AT 40: Wolfgang Puck was branching out in the Bay Area. Having immigrated to America from Europe at age 24, the chef had already achieved fame in his 30s with his Los Angeles eatery, Spago, and its anything-goes California cuisine. (Duck-sausage pizza, anyone?) Not content to show himself as a one-trick pony, he opened a restaurant in San Francisco, adapting the city's cuisine into his wacky style. Several years later, diners in airports across America would be able to enjoy his flatbread creation at Wolfgang Puck Express eateries.

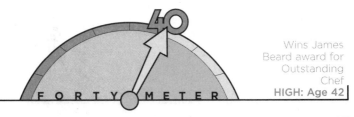

Tops pizza with only cheese and tomato sauce (unconfirmed)
LOW: Age 29

FORTYMETER

Wins James Beard award for Outstanding Chef
HIGH: Age 42

Turned 40: 2/4/1953
Profession: Mother of a movement
Length of Montgomery bus boycott: 382 days

PARKS WAS ON HER FEET

AT 40: Respected in the black community of Montgomery, Alabama, for her work with the local voters league and the NAACP, Rosa Parks was fighting discrimination quietly. Instead of riding in a segregated elevator, she took the stairs. Instead of taking public transportation, sometimes she walked. But by age 42, she was ready to make noise. Her refusal to move to the back of a Montgomery city bus that year was the spark that ignited the Civil Rights movement.

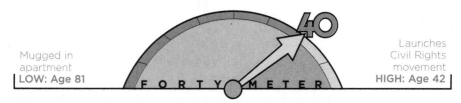

Mugged in
apartment
LOW: Age 81

FORTY METER

Launches
Civil Rights
movement
HIGH: Age 42

Turned 40: 8/27/1950
Profession: Mother to millions
Trained in: Dublin, Ireland

MOTHER TERESA | POPE'D UP

AT 40: Two years after leaving a convent in Calcutta, India, where she taught high school, Mother Teresa received permission from Pope Pius XII to start her own order, The Missionaries of Charity. The Pope's blessing of her work with the city's poor, which still lacked significant funds, enabled Teresa to broaden her aid to those most in need. At age 69, Teresa would be named again—this time as the winner of the Nobel Peace Prize.

Savaged in Christopher Hitchens book
LOW: Age 85

Wins Nobel Peace Prize
HIGH: Age 69

FORTY METER

JERRY RICE
Turned 40: 10/13/2002

KEPT STREAKING

The NFL's all time leading receiver turned 40 in style, catching seven passes for 133 yards against the St. Louis Rams. Reborn as an Oakland Raider, Rice had his best season since he was a young lad of 34.

GORDIE HOWE
Turned 40: 3/31/1968

SKATED INTO MIDDLE AGE

After more than 20 years in pro hockey, Howe had his best season at the age of 41 when he tallied 44 goals and 59 assists for the Detroit Red Wings. Eleven years later, he was still skating, playing in every game of the 1979–80 season.

JANET GUTHRIE
Turned 40: 3/7/1978

GOT REVVED UP

A year after becoming the first woman to compete in the Indianapolis 500 and Daytona 500, Guthrie, who owned and managed her own team, raced to a ninth-place finish in the Indianapolis 500 at age 40. Her performance remains the best by a woman at Indy.

MARTINA NAVRATILOVA **Turned 40:** 10/18/1996
DITCHED THE WOODEN RACKET

Thirteen years removed from her last Grand Slam singles title, 46-year-old Navratilova became the oldest Grand Slam champion in tennis history when she won the Australian Open mixed doubles title with Leander Paes. Later that year, she served-and-volleyed her way to another Slam in the Wimbledon mixed doubles.

MICHAEL JORDAN **Turned 40:** 2/17/2003
INDUCED FLASHBACKS

Four days after his 40th birthday, Jordan dropped 40 points on the Nets, become the first NBA player to score 40 at 40. He averaged 20 points, 6.1 rebounds, and 3.8 points for the season, his last, but failed to carry the Washington Wizards to the playoffs.

"There's definitely going to be more 40-year-old pro athletes. I wouldn't be surprised if someday we see a 45-year-old running back in the NFL."

—Dr. Richard Kreider,
Head of the Center for Exercise, Nutrition and
Preventive Health Research at Baylor University

CHAPTER 6

"At the age of 20, we don't care what the world thinks of us;
at 30, we worry about what it is thinking of us;
at 40, we discover that it wasn't thinking of us at all."

—*Anonymous*

LIFE ENDS AT 40

Okay, so you're fat, bald, and in need of a facelift. Sometimes, you have trouble remembering stuff. But things could be a lot worse. Consider the case of the Truskese of Micronesia, who believe that life quite literally ends at 40, as noted by anthropologist J. T. Gire: "When you reach 40, you are, in effect, dead. Given the physically demanding activities engaged in by people in this society, there seems to be a noticeable decline in the ability of the Truskese to perform their socially assigned roles at acceptable standards at this age. Sensing that the end must be coming, the individual begins to prepare for death and is viewed as being dead even before he or she transitions to that point as viewed from the Western perspective." (Note to publisher: Cancel Micronesian book release party.)

MOST SHOCKING REVELATION

Ron Jeremy gets bit parts. (p. 164)

LEAST SHOCKING REVELATION

Falco only had one #1 song. (p. 156)

TALK ABOUT SECOND ACTS!

Moses was forced into an early retirement from his post as a palace exec in Egypt (bad temper). He bounced around for 40 years or so, until he was rehired and led the Exodus.

DATA OMITTED

Data: By 40, your aortic glands have disappeared
Reason Omitted: Didn't know we had 'em!

Data: Elvis is the top-ranked "dead earner"
Reason Omitted: Elvis is alive

Data: "When you reach forty you can't do anything every day."
–Henry "Hank" Aaron
Omitted: Words of a classic underachiever

CHAPTER QUIZ

1. Which of the following nicknames has Jesse Ventura used?
a. "The Body"
b. "The Mind"
c. "The Soul"
d. "The Hairpiece"

2. TRUE OR FALSE?
Your bone density is thinner than your hair.

3. ESSAY QUESTION
Reminisce about the oldest ox you have known.

YOUR BEST YEARS ARE BEHIND YOU

By 40, your body has begun its slow fade to the grave

"40 is the old age of youth." —*Victor Hugo*

"It may be true that life begins at 40, but everything else starts to wear out, fall out, or spread out." —*Beryl Pfizer*

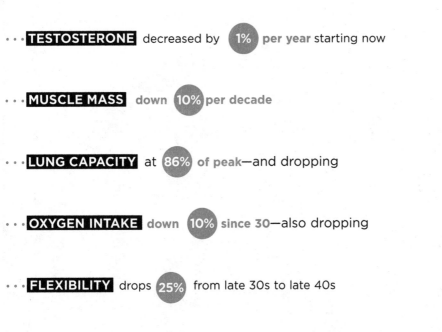

··· **TESTOSTERONE** decreased by 1% per year starting now

··· **MUSCLE MASS** down 10% per decade

··· **LUNG CAPACITY** at 86% of peak—and dropping

··· **OXYGEN INTAKE** down 10% since 30—also dropping

··· **FLEXIBILITY** drops 25% from late 30s to late 40s

HAIR TODAY, GONE TOMORROW

 of men **are balding** by 40

40% of 40-year-olds **have gray hair**

"When forty winters shall besiege thy brow..." —*William Shakespeare*

55% of Botox injections

45% **OF ALL COSMETIC PROCEDURES** are performed on late 30s and 40somethings

37% of breast augmentations

62% of tummy tucks

44% of collagen injections

47% of liposuctions

male chest enhancements **57%**

LIFE EXPECTANCY FOR 40-YEAR-OLDS 79.2 years

FOR MEN 77.0

FOR WOMEN 81.3

most common ways to die at age 40

18% CANCER

17% ACCIDENTS

15% HEART DISEASE

7% SUICIDE

7% HIV

PAGING MR. REAPER

famous folks who passed away at 40

JOHN COLTRANE
JAZZ MUSICIAN

40: 9/23/1966

Having established himself as a creative force to be reckoned with in the jazz world with his three-on-one chord approach and "sheets of sound"—a method of playing multiple notes at one time on the sax—"The Trane" succumbed to liver cancer at age 40.

JACK LONDON
AUTHOR, *THE CALL OF THE WILD*

Turned 40: 1/2/1916

The official cause of death for the *Call of the Wild* writer was gastrointestinal uremia, but it is speculated he really died of a self-administered overdose of morphine. At the time of his death, though he was one of the most popular authors of his time, London couldn't shake the fear that he was losing his creativity.

FALCO
ROCK STAR

Turned 40: 2/19/1997

The songster died 12 days shy of his 41st birthday when he drove his SUV into a bus. Though Falco had not had a number one hit since "Rock Me Amadeus" 11 years earlier, it is hard not to feel that New Wave German pop music lost one of its greats on that day.

LENNY BRUCE
Turned 40: 10/13/1965

COMEDIAN AND TROUBLEMAKER

Constant run-ins with the authorities over drugs and obscenity had left the comedian born Leonard Alfred Schneider broke and unemployable by age 40. (Bruce claimed that the cops threatened to bust any club owner who allowed him to perform.) Two months before his 41st birthday, he was found dead of a drug overdose on the floor of his Hollywood home.

PETE MARAVICH
Turned 40: 6/22/1947

BASKETBALL GREAT

The top scorer in NCAA basketball history—he averaged 44.5 points a game as a senior at LSU—and a 10-year NBA star, Maravich sunk his last basket during a pickup game in a California gym. A heart attack put Maravich on permanent timeout.

GLENN MILLER
Turned 40: 3/1/1944

BIG BAND IMPRESARIO

Convinced that he could modernize the military band and improve soldier morale, the "Tuxedo Junction" big band leader had enlisted at age 38. The Glenn Miller Air Force Band was preparing for a six-week European tour when Miller boarded a flight to the City of Lights. His plane disappeared somewhere over the English Channel.

Turned 40: 9/24/1936
Profession: Novelist
Generation: Lost

F. SCOTT FITZGERALD
WENT HOLLYWOOD

BREAKTHROUGH: At 24, Fitzgerald became the darling of the literary set with the publication of his first novel, *This Side of Paradise.* A week after the book's release, he married Zelda Sayre.

BREAKDOWN: By 40, Fitzgerald had entered his self-described "crack-up" phase. Zelda was institutionalized, his daughter was living with a surrogate family, debt was piling up, and the booze was flowing. So he went to Hollywood to write films for MGM for $1,000 a week. Alas, there was no second act for Fitzgerald. MGM declined to renew his contract, and Fitzgerald died of a heart attack two years later.

Turned 40: 10/9/1980
Profession: The Smart One
Favorite Beatles: John, Ringo (tie)

JOHN LENNON
BECAME THE DEAD ONE

BREAKTHROUGH: After a rough period in the mid-'70s during which he had been separated, addicted, and almost deported, Lennon's personal life was on the upswing. At 39, he unretired and recorded *Double Fantasy* with Yoko Ono. The album, released when Lennon was 40, was a moderate hit.

BREAKDOWN: On December 8, 1980, Lennon was shot by a crazed fan outside his New York City apartment. Six days later, he died. *Double Fantasy* shot up to number one on the charts. Ironically, John had written a song entitled "Life Begins at 40" for Ringo Starr's album *Stop and Smell the Roses,* but it was never used.

Turned 40: 1/8/1975
Profession: Hunka hunka burnin' love
Cost of first guitar (age 12): $12.75

ELVIS PRESLEY
PASSED ON GRACELESSLY

BREAKTHROUGH: Though he still played to sellout crowds across the country, including frequent appearances at Vegas casinos, Presley turned to overeating and prescription drugs in his 30s to mask his pain and paranoia.

BREAKDOWN: By 40, Elvis had all but left the building for the final time. At 38, his wife, Priscilla, had divorced him, leaving him alone in his Graceland mansion—and under the thumb of his autocratic manager, Colonel Tom Parker. At age 42, Presley would be found in his bathroom, dead of a drug overdose—unless, of course, that was Elvis we saw at the • • • • minimart down the street last week.

"Legendary Elvis Presley overwhelmed 22,000 devoted fans in the Richfield Coliseum last night and showed them that life really does begin at 40. At least for Elvis it does. Sure, his white-sequined jump suit is a couple of sizes larger these days. And granted his blue-black hair is a bit thinner, and even his most worshipping fan will admit he doesn't shake it like he used to. But his voice never sounded better, and that's what made him king of rock n' roll for more than 20 years."

—*Cleveland Press, 1976*

31% of 40somethings call themselves Elvis fans

43% of 40somethings have danced to an Elvis song

10% of 40somethings have visited Graceland

6% of 40somethings have tried to impersonate Elvis

OVER THE (HOLLYWOOD) HILL
showbiz declines after 40

DEBRA WINGER
Turned 40: 5/16/1995

WALKED AWAY

Though she was as celebrated as any actress of her era, with three Oscar nominations under her belt by the time she turned 40, Debra Winger quit the Hollywood rat race at 40. At the time, she told a British newspaper, "Nothing quite compares with the sense of liberation I felt. It stays with me: I am happy and I am free."

> "People under the age of 40 are favored in the entertainment industry. More than twice as many roles were cast with actors who were under the age of 40 than actors who were 40 or over."
>
> —*Screen Actors Guild*

KEVIN COSTNER
Turned 40: 1/18/1995

GOT LOST AT SEA

As 40 dawned, things didn't look so bad for Kevin Costner. He was just four years removed from a Best Director/Best Picture double for *Dances with Wolves* and a few more from *Bull Durham, Field of Dreams,* and *The Untouchables.* Then came *Waterworld,* a big budget flop of titanic proportions. Costner's ship sunk fast: *The Postman,* anybody? *Tin Cup?*

Alexander Turned 40: 9/23/1999
Dreyfus Turned 40: 1/13/2001
Richards Turned 40: 7/24/1989
Seinfeld Turned 40: 4/29/1994

JERRY'S BUDDIES
WERE CURSED

At the end of the final episode of *Seinfeld*, Jerry and the gang were sentenced to prison. In real life, they didn't fair much better. Over the course of three years, Alexander, at 42 (*Bob Patterson*), Louis-Dreyfus, at 41 (*Watching Ellie*), and Richards, at 51 (*The Michael Richards Show*), all bombed in their own TV vehicles. With each successive failure, the buzz about the "Seinfeld Curse" grew louder. Finally, Alexander put that all to rest with some superb work as "The Chicken Man" in a series of KFC commercials.

REDEMPTION SONG
climbing back on top after 40

RON JEREMY
Turned 40: 2/24/1985
WENT FROM XXX TO EXTRA

With hundreds of XXX-rated classics (see *Attack of the Monster, Mammaries, Gazongas*) under his, er, belt, Jeremy attempted to break into clothed acting in his late 40s. Despite bit parts in *Toxic Avenger 4, Detroit Rock City* and *Fast Sofa* and cameos galore, the transition has been slow. But Jeremy's starring role in the biopic *Porn Star: The Legend of Ron Jeremy,* at age 49 finally brought him to a wide audience

SONNY BONO
Turned 40: 2/16/1975
STOPPED CHERING

With the popularity of *Sonny & Cher* on the decline, 40-year-old Bono made his solo acting debut in the TV movie *Murder on Flight 503.* At age 47, he changed careers, opening the West Hollywood restaurant BONO. Then, at 53, he registered to vote for the first time and switched to politics, winning the office of Mayor of Palm Springs.

JESSE VENTURA
Turned 40: 7/15/1991
ENTERED ANOTHER ARENA

After injuries forced "The Body" to retire from wrestling in his early 30s, Ventura turned to Hollywood, landing a role in *Predator.* At 39, he gave up fake blood altogether and ran for mayor of Brooklyn Park, Minnesota. He won, and took office at 40. Seven years later, he was elected governor of the state.

JOHN TRAVOLTA
Turned 40: 2/18/1994
RETURNED TO MAKING HITS

Once the hottest thing in a skin-tight white disco suit, Travolta spent his 30s starring in *Look Who's Talking, Look Who's Talking Too,* and *Look Who's Talking Now.* Just when it looked like Tony Manero would have to do another epic of wit and drool, Quentin Tarantino gave the 40-year-old Travolta the lead in *Pulp Fiction* and made him the hottest thing in an extra-large black gangster suit.

CANDICE BERGEN
Turned 40: 5/9/1986
WAS NO DUMMY

Thanks to her ventriloquist father, Bergen was famous before she left the womb. Eventually, she developed her own voice: at at 33, she earned an Oscar nod for *Starting Over.* But a handful of TV movies threatened to stall her ascent. Then, at 42, she landed the part of Murphy Brown. Four years later, she was sparring with Dan Quayle over abortion rights.

BETTE MIDLER
Turned 40: 12/1/1985
GOT HER WIND BACK

By the time she was 30, The Divine Miss M was a triple-threat star. But after the 34-year-old Midler was nominated for an Oscar (for *The Rose*), things started to sour. Her next film bombed, she had a nervous breakdown, and nobody wanted anything to do with her. But out of tragedy, came comedy! At 41, she returned to the screen in *Down and Out in Beverly Hills.* At 43, she produced and starred in *Beaches,* singing the tear-jerking theme ("The Wind Beneath My Wings").

What are the odds you'll live to see **YOUR LATE FORTIES?** · · · · · ·

SOURCES

AS REGARDS "EARLY 40S" AND "40S"

Throughout this book, "early 40s" refers to ages 40-44 and "40s" refers to ages 40-49, unless otherwise noted below.

Keanu Reeves quote from "Men at 40," *Extra*, Nov. 3, 2003.

p. 5: Definition from *The New Oxford American Dictionary*, Oxford University Press, 2001.

CHAPTER 1: YOU ARE 40

p. 5-7: Jung quote from Spiritualityhealth. com. Dr. Phil quote from "Dr. Phil's Ten Life Laws," DrPhil.com. Internet stats from "More Than One-Third of Internet Users Now Have Broadband," The Harris Poll #3, Jan. 14, 2004. Snoring stats from *Understanding Snoring and Sleep Apnea*, Yale University Press via the *Jerusalem Post*. Belgium stats from *The World Factbook 2003*. Hoffman details from the Internet Movie Database (www.IMDb.com—hereafter referenced as IMDb).

p. 9: Stats from U.S. Census 2000 (www.census.gov). Number of Americans turning 40 "this year" based on the total number of 36-year-olds in 2000 who are presumably turning 40 in 2004. The number of "Americans in their 40s" based on the total number of 36- to 45-year-olds in 2000 who are presumably in the 30-39 age group in 2004.

p. 10: Stats from U.S. Census 2000; median income stats are ages 35-44.

p. 11: Height and weight stats from workerscompensation.com.

p. 12: Stats from Edward O. Laumann, John H. Gagnon, Robert T. Michael, and Stuart Michaels, *The Social Organization of Sexuality: Sexual Practices in the United States*, The University of Chicago Press, 2000, p. 356.

p. 13: Type of apple: Macintosh. Crunch: excellent. Taste: delicious.

p. 14: Stats from Bureau of Labor Statistics, "Monthly Labor Review," Bureau of Labor Statistics, May 2002.

p. 15: Promotion stats from "Number of Jobs Held, Labor Market Activity, and Earnings Growth Over Two Decades: Results from a Longitudinal Survey," U.S. Department of Labor, Bureau of Labor Statistics, August 2002. Stats are for employed individuals ages 35-43 who were promoted between 1997 and 1999. Unemployment stat from "Employment Status of the Civilian Noninstitutional Population," Bureau of Labor Statistics, 2003.

p. 16: Stats from "The Religious and Other Beliefs of Americans 2003," The Harris Poll #11, February 26, 2003 (www.harrisinteractive.com); stats are ages 40-49.

p. 17: Stats from "While Most Americans Believe in God, Only 36% Attend a Religious Service Once a Month or More Often," The Harris Poll #59, October 15, 2003; stats are ages 40-49.

p. 18: Quote from *University of Washington Health Beat* via "Exercising Caution over 40," www.lifeclinic.com. Men's fitness stats from Adam Campbell, "A Fit Man Can...," Men's Health (www.menshealth.com). Women's fitness stats from "Shape Your Best Life Fitness Tests," *Shape* (www.shape.com), April 2002. Stats are for

40-year-olds; run stats in minutes. The "1.5 Mile Run" is described in *Shape* as "1.5 Mile Walk/Run Cardio Test," with, alas, no clarification offered as to what that is.

p. 19: First two stats from "Smoking, Obesity, and Not Using Seat Belts Much More Common Among People with the Least Education," The Harris Poll #15, Mar. 3, 1999. Third stat from National Health and Nutrition Examination Survey, CDC, 1994. Quote from Council on Size & Weight Discrimination (www.cswd.org).

p. 20-21: Quote from "On dining with the abstinent King Ibn Saud of Saudi Arabia," *Triumph and Tragedy*, Houghton Mifflin, 53. Stats from "National Survey on Drug Use and Health," Substance Abuse and Mental Health Services Administration, Office of Applied Studies, 2002 (www.samhsa.gov).

p. 22: Quote from Constance J. Jones and William Meredith, "Development Paths of Psychological Health from Early Adolescence to Later Adulthood," *Psychology and Aging*, Vol. 15, No. 2, 2000.

p. 23: Stats from Laumann et al., T*he Social Organization of Sexuality: Sexual Practices in the United States*, The University of Chicago Press, 2000. Quote from Schizophrenia.com. Stats are for age 40-49.

p. 24: Stats from Tom W. Smith, "2001 National Gun Policy Survey of the National Opinion Research Center: Research Findings," National Opinion Research Center, University of Chicago, December 2001. Stats are for ages 40-49.

p. 25: Stats from "Gun Ownership: Two in Five Americans Live in Gun-Owning Households," The Harris Poll #25, May 30, 2001. Results in response to the question,

"Do you happen to have in your home or garage any guns or revolvers? If yes; "Do you have a pistol or not?" "Do you have a shotgun or not?" "Do you have a rifle or not?"

p. 26: Stats from "Huge Differences Between Values of Young Adults and Older Adults," The Harris Poll #58, Oct. 4, 2000. Results in response to the question "People have different ideas about what's right and wrong. As I read things some people do, tell me whether you think each one is absolutely wrong under all circumstances, wrong under most but not all circumstances, wrong only sometimes, or not wrong at all."

p. 27: Quote from Marcus Aurelius, *Meditations*, 2nd century. Music stats from "Americans Think Downloading Music for Personal Use Is an Innocent Act," The Harris Poll #5, January 28, 2004. Results in response to the question "There has been a lot of news lately about what some are calling 'Internet music piracy.' Please tell me if you agree or disagree with the following statement: Downloading music off the Internet is no different from buying a used CD or recording music borrowed from a friend." Tattoo stats from "A Third of Americans with Tattoos Say They Make Them Feel More Sexy," The Harris Poll #58, October 8, 2003. Results in response to the questions "How many tattoos do you currently have on your body?" and "Please complete the following sentence: "Compared to not having a tattoo...having a tattoo has made me feel...?" Answers to later question were not broken out by age.

p. 28-29: Stats from respondents to a poll on Queer Astrology (www.gay-astrology.com), Mar. 2004. Results in response to the questions "How old were you when you first realized you were gay/lesbian/TG?" and "How old were you when you came out of the closet?"

p. 30-31: Stats from "Educational Attainment: 2000," U.S. Census Bureau, August 2000. Quote from *Love of Fame*. Satire ii. Line 28.

p. 32-33: Stats from "Housing Vacancies and Homeownership Annual Statistics: 2002," U.S. Census.

CHAPTER 2: LIFE BEGINS AT 40

p. 35-37: Lennon quote via John-Lennon.com. "Your life is changing yet again..." quote from beauty.about.com. *Jeffersons* lyrics from www.lyricsonde-mand.com.

p. 38-39: Details from Kaplan, James, "Angry Middle-Aged Man," *The New Yorker*, 1/19/04; IMDb; HBO.com.

p. 40: Details from Hollywood.com; IMDb

p. 41: Details from BBC World Service (www.bbc.co.uk); newadvent.org.

p. 42-43: Details from IMDb and movie press materials.

p. 44: Details from IMDb; Cosmo's Factory (www.cosmosfactory.com).

p. 45: Details from IMDb. Quote from The Quotations Page (www.quotationspage.com).

p. 46-47: Stowe details from AmericanCivilWar.com. Ludlum details from BarnesandNoble.com. Cervantes from The Literature Network (www.online-literature.com). Vonnegut details from Frank Houston, "The Salon Interview: Kurt Vonnegut," Salon.com, Oct. 8, 1999 and

Kurt-Vonnegut.com. Crace details from Dave Welch, " Jim Crace Peels Off the Labels," Powells.com; "Jim Crace: Reasons to be cheerful," *The Independent*, Sept. 6, 2003; British Council, ContemporaryWriters.org). Shields from "Pulitzer Prize Winner Carol Shields Dies," CBC News, July 18, 2003; "Human Shield," *The Observer Magazine*, Apr. 28, 2002.

p. 48: Details from The History Place (www.historyplace.com)

p. 50: Details from Emily Eaken, "Jonathan Franzen's Big Book," *The New York Times Magazine*, September 2, 2001. Quote from "Mainstream and Meaningful," *The Atlantic*, Oct. 3, 2001.

p. 51: Details from "Novelist James Michener Dies," CNN.com; Academy of Achievement (www.achievement.org).

p. 52: Details from Alex Witchel, "Sonoma's Chuck Williams: He Changed the Way America Cooks," Associated Press, Feb. 11, 2004.

p. 53: Details from Satchel Paige: The Official Website (www.cmgww.com).

p. 55: Details from the Baseball Almanac (www.baseball-almanac.com).

CHAPTER 3: LOVE, SEX, & FAMILY AT 40

p. 57-59: Thackeray quote from William Makepeace Thackeray, *The Age of Wisdom* (no later than 1863). Dr. Brothers quote from "Dr. Joyce Brothers, "Why Screen Heroes Are Usually Older Than Their Women," Syndicated, Feb. 6, 2004. "Burnout" quote from "Dealing with Specific Sexual Problems," MentalHelp.net. Scientists stat from Nicholas Wade, "Prime Numbers: What

Science and Crime Have in Common," *The New York Times,* July 27, 2003. Second divorce stats from "Number, Timing, and Duration of Marriages and Divorces: 1996," U.S. Census Bureau, Feb. 2002. Orgasm stats from "National Health and Social Life Survey," National Opinion Research Center, 1992.

p. 60-62: Stats from "Number, Timing, and Duration of Marriages and Divorces: 1996," U.S. Census Bureau, Feb. 2002.

p. 63: Stats from "Marital Status and Living Arrangements: March 1998 (Update)," U.S. Census Bureau, Dec. 1998.

p. 64-65: Taylor details from Swingin' Chicks of the '60s (www.swinginchicks.com) and IMDb. Cortes details from "Bigamy Bride a Single Mother," *New York Post,* Jan. 8, 2004. Clooney details from IMDb. Jackson details from MTV.com and BBC.co.uk. Bushnell details from "Sex and the City Creator Marries," BBC.co.uk, July 8, 2002.

p. 66-67: "Fertility, Family Planning, and Women's Health: New Data from the 1995 National Survey of Family Growth," Centers for Disease Control and Prevention/National Center for Health Statistics, May 1997. Quote from *Saturday Evening Post,* Dec. 1, 1962.

p. 68: Quote from Katy Abel, "Worth the Wait: Parenthood at 40-Plus," FamilyEducation.com.

p. 69: Stats from U.S. Census.

p. 70-71: Davis details from IMDb. Iman details from I-Iman.com. Bening details from IMDb. Thompson details from Bruce Kirkland, "Emma Digs Deep," *Toronto Sun,* Nov. 6, 2003, IMDb. Madonna details from IMDb.

p. 72-73: Stendahl quote from *The Unabridged William Shakespeare,* William George Clark and William Aldis Wright, eds., Running Press, 1989.Shaw quote from *Man and Superman,* "The Revolutionist's Handbook," *The Bodley Head Bernard Shaw: Collected Plays with their Prefaces,* vol. 2, Dan H. Laurence ed., 1971. Stats from "Number, Timing, and Duration of Marriages and Divorces: 1996," U.S. Census Bureau, Feb. 2002.

p. 74-75: Stella details from HowStella.com; IMDb.

p. 76-81: Stats from James A. Davis, Peter V. Marsden, and Tom W. Smith, General Social Survey 1972-2000, cumulative 3rd version, National Opinion Research Center, Chicago, Illinois, 2001. Extracted from the data file stored at sda.berkeley.edu; stats are for ages 35-44 covering sexual activity since 18. Stats inside circles on pp. 78-79 from Laumann et al., *The Social Organization of Sexuality: Sexual Practices in the United States,* The University of Chicago Press, 2000, p. 305.

MIDLIFE CRISIS INTERLUDE

p. 82-83: Is It Real? data from "Medicare's Midlife Crisis," The Cato Institute, Nov. 2001; Oh, It's Real data from Sue Shellenbarger, "The Lows and Highs Of a Midlife Crisis," *The Wall Street Journal,* Aug. 15, 2003.

p. 84-85: IMDb.

p. 86-87: Ask Carl quotes from Carl Jung, "The Stages of Life" from *Modern Man In Search of a Soul,* 1933; The Bad News from Gail Sheehy, *Passages,* 1976. The Good News data from "41 Is the 'Ideal Age,'" The Harris Poll #61, October 22, 2003; Secunda quote from Victoria Secunda, *Women and Their*

Fathers, ch. 4, 1992; Cooley quote from Mason Cooley, *City Aphorisms*, Fourth Selection, New York, 1987; Reagan quote from *The Washington Post*, Feb. 7, 1977; Molineux quote from "Surviving The Mid-Life Crisis," SolveYourProblem.com.

CHAPTER 4: MONEY & POWER AT 40

p. 89-91: Martin Luther quote from Martin Luther, *Table Talk*, 1546. Collection letter quote based on prose from SendSnailmail.com. Drill sergeant details from Staff Sgt. Marcia Triggs, "Army Ups Max Age to 40 for Drill Sergeants," Army News Service, June 25, 2002.

p. 92: Stats from "Employee Tenure in 2002," Bureau of Labor Statistics, Dec. 2002.

p. 93: Stats from U.S. Census Bureau, 2000.

p. 94: Details from "Henry Ford Museum: America's Greatest History Attraction," www.hfmgv.org.

p. 95: Stats from Arthur B. Kennickell, Martha Starr-McClurer, and Brian J. Surette, "Recent Changes in U.S. Family Finances: Results from the 1998 Survey of Consumer Finances," Federal Reserve Bulletin, Jan. 2000; value is median; stat is families with head of household ages 36-45.

p. 96: Stats from "Kids and Careers," JA Interprise Poll, Junior Achievement Inc., Jan. 15, 2004.

p. 97-99: Savings and net worth stats from Ana M. Aizcorbe et al., "Recent Changes in U.S. Family Finances: Evidence from the 1998 and 2001 Survey of Consumer Finances," Federal Reserve Bulletin, Jan. 2003; stats are for families with head of

household between 35 and 44 years old and values are median. Average expected retirement stats from "3.7 Million People Over 55 Not Working Now Are Ready, Willing and Able to Work," The Harris Poll #62, Mar. 17, 1999. Results in response to the question "At what age do you expect to stop working in a paid job?"

p. 100: Details from John Huey, "The Time 100: Sam Walton," *Time*, Dec. 7, 1998.

p. 101: Details from Michael Bloomberg, *Bloomberg by Bloomberg*, John Wiley & Sons, Inc., 1997; nyc.gov.

p. 102-103: Stats from Ana M. Aizcorbe et al., "Recent Changes in U.S. Family Finances: Evidence from the 1998 and 2001 Survey of Consumer Finances," Federal Reserve Bulletin, Jan. 2003; stats are for families with head of household between 35 and 44 years old and values are median.

p. 105: Quote from "Overview of Aging and Accessible Technology," Microsoft.com; Internet stats from "More Than One-Third of Internet Users Now Have Broadband," The Harris Poll #3, Jan. 14, 2004. Results in response to questions "At home, do you personally use a computer to access the Internet/World Wide Web?", "At work, do you personally use a computer to access the Internet/World Wide Web?", and "At another location, do you personally use a computer to access the Internet/World Wide Web?". Discrimination stats from Shelly K. Schwartz, "Careers After Retirement," CNNfn, June 9, 1999.

p. 106: Stats from Voting and Registration in the Election of November 2000," U.S. Census Bureau, Feb. 27, 2002. Quote from Ben Franklin, *Poor Richard's Almanac*, June 1741.

p. 107: Stats from "Top 5 Youngest Presidents," Time for Kids, Nov. 17, 2000; DePaul University Quantitative Reasoning Center.

p. 108: Details from Project Vote Smart (www.vote-smart.org); JohnKerry.com; The Center for Public Integrity (www.publicintegrity.org)

p. 109: Details from The Center for Public Integrity (www.publicintegrity.org); Details from Richard Brookhiser, "Close-Up: The Mind of George W. Bush," *The Atlantic*, March 2003, whitehouse.gov; Project Vote Smart (www.vote-smart.org).

p. 110-111: Reagan details from The Reagan Foundation (www.reaganfoundation.org); IMDb. Washington details from "George Washington," Supercomputing '94 Tour (sc94.ameslab.gov); Kennedy details from whitehouse.gov. Nixon details from whitehouse.gov; AmericanPresident.org. Roosevelt details from Edmund Morris, *The Rise of Theodore Roosevelt*, The Modern Library, 1979.

p. 112: Details from The Official Mahatma Gandhi eArchive & Reference Library, Mahatma Gandhi Foundation (web.mahatma.org.in).

p. 113: Details from The Legacy of Genghis Khan (www.lacma.org).

p. 114-115: Thatcher details from Paul Johnson, "Leaders & Revolutionaries: Margaret Thatcher," Time 100, Time.com. Mao details from the Maoist Documentation Project (www.maoism.org). Napoleon details from PBS Online. Isabella details from TheHistoryNet (www.thehistorynet.com). Mandela details from www.anc.org.za and Nobel.se. Blair details from ABCNews.com.

CHAPTER 5: FORTYMETER

p. 117-119: Schopenhauer quote via useful-information.com. Dunne quote from Finley Peter Dunne, Dooley's Opinions, "Casual Observations," 1901.

p. 120: Details from IMDb. Quote from "Men at 40," *Extra*, Nov. 3, 2003.

p. 122: Details from The Museum of Broadcast Communications (www.museum.tv).

p. 123: Details from The Museum of Broadcast Communications (www.museum.tv).

p. 124: Details from InfoVoyager: Explorers Guide to Information (infopedia.ruv.net); Guggenheim Museum (www.guggenheimcollection.org); Olga's Gallery (www.abcgallery.com); The Art Institute of Chicago (www.artic.edu).

p. 125: Details from artelino (www.artelino.com); Nuhn Fine Art (www.andywarholart.com). Quote from BrainyQuote (www.brainyquote.com).

p. 126: Details from Oprah.com and CNN.com.

p. 127: Details from SpringerShow.com; IMDb. Quote from "Jerry Springer—The Opera," *CBS News Sunday Morning*, Nov. 16, 2003.

p. 128: Details from Alan Lightman, "Relativity and the Cosmos," NOVA online (www.pbs.org).

p. 129: Details from NASA; The John and Annie Glenn Historic Site and Exploration Center (www.johnglennhome.org). Quote from BrainyQuote.

p. 131: Details from IMDb.

p. 132: Details from "The List: The Best 40-Somethings," ESPN Page 2 (espn.go.com/page2); Big George Foreman's Place (www.biggeorge.com); boxing.about.com.

p. 133: Details from IMDb; All Music Guide (www.allmusic.com).

p. 134: Details from Academy of Achievement: A Museum of Living History (www.achievement.org); Wilfrid Sheed, "The Time 100: Jonas Salk," *Time*, March 29, 1999; "Sabin vs. Salk: Oral vs. Injected Vaccine—Polio: Combating the Crippler," CBC Archives, Jul. 6, 1977.

p. 135: Details from The Paul Revere House (www.paulreverehouse.org); InfoPlease (www.infoplease.com); Lyrics from "Paul Revere," Beastie Boys via Sing365.com.

p. 136: Details from IMDb; EverythingCher.com. Quote from Divas The Site (www.divasthesite.com).

p. 137: Details from Sing365.com and IMDb.

p. 138-139: Album and biography details from All Music Guide; Jagger details from AskMen.com. Turner details from www.tina-turner.com. Springsteen details from Backstreets.com.

p. 140: Details from "The List: The Best 40-Somethings," ESPN Page 2; Nolan Ryan Express (www.nolanryan.net).

p. 141: Details from StarPulse.com and WolfgangPuck.com.

p. 142-143: Details from TheGlassCeiling.com.

p. 144-145: Rice details from John Donovan, "Life at 40," CNNSI, Jan 23, 2003; "The List: The Best 40-Somethings," ESPN Page 2. Howe details from Hockey Fans (www.hockey-fans.com); "The List: The Best 40-Somethings," ESPN Page 2. Guthrie details from JanetGuthrie.com. Navratilova details from Phil Brown, "Navratilova Becomes Oldest Grand Slam Champion," *USA Today*, Jan. 25, 2003. Jordan details from Steve Wyche, "Good, Old Jordan," *Washington Post*, Feb 17, 2003; CBS Sportsline. Quote from Martin Miller, "Raising the Bar at 40," *Los Angeles Times*, Sept. 29, 2003.

CHAPTER 6: LIFE ENDS AT 40

p. 147-149: Anonymous quote from ThinkExist.com; Micronesians quote from J. T. Gire, "How Death Imitates Life: Cultural Influences on C onceptions of Death and Dying," 2002 in W. J. Lonner, D. L. Dinnel, S. A. Hayes, & D. N. Sattler (Eds.), *Online Readings in Psychology and Culture* (Unit 14, Chapter 2); Aortic glands data from Henry Gray, *Anatomy of the Human Body*, 1918; Elvis data from Forbes.com; Aaron quote from Brain Candy (www.corsinet.com).

p. 150-151: Stat 1 from "After 40, Dropping Testosterone Levels May Affect Health," NYT Syndicate, April 25, 2000. Stats 2,3,5 from Edmund Burke, "Will Aging Air Jordan Still Be Able to Fly?" *USA Today*, Oct. 30, 2001. Stat 4 from OxygenForHealth.com.

p. 152: Stats from "Aging Changes in Hair and Nails," Yahoo! Health; Propecia-Pharmacy.com. Quote from Lord Warburton in Henry James, *The Portrait of a Lady*.

p. 153: Stats from The American Society for Aesthetic Plastic Surgery, Cosmetic Surgery National Data Bank, 2003 Statistics. Quote from William Shakespeare, "When forty winters shall besiege thy brow (l. 1-14)" in *The Unabridged William Shakespeare*, William George Clark and William Aldis Wright, eds., Running Press, 1989.

p. 154: Stats from Elizabeth Arias, "National Vital Statistics Reports: United States Life

Tables 2001," Vol. 52, No. 14, Center for Disease Control, Feb. 18, 2004. Stats are for 40-year-olds.

p. 155: Stats from Robert N. Anderson, Ph.D., "Deaths: Leading Causes for 2000," Division of Vital Statistics from "National Vital Statistic Report," Volume 50, Number 16, Sept. 16, 2002.

p. 156-157: Details from DeadorAlive.com. London details from The Literature Network (www.online-literature.com). Coltrane details from JohnColtrane.com. Bruce details from IMDb. Miller details from GlennMiller Orchestra.com; Maravich details from The Basketball Hall of Fame (www.hoophall.com); NBA.com. Falco Details from All Music Guide.

p. 158: Details from "A Brief Life of Fitzgerald," University of South Carolina (www.sc.edu).

p. 159: Details from RollingStone.com.

p. 161: Quote via ElvisConcerts.com. Stats from "Elvis Presley Has Touched the Lives of the Vast Majority of Americans," The Harris Poll #39, Aug. 12, 2002.

p. 162: Winger details James L. Hirsen, "Vintage Hollywood Whine," Newsmax.com, Aug. 4, 2002. Costner details from IMDb.

p. 163: *Seinfeld* details from IMDb.

p. 164-165: Jeremy details from IMDb. Bono details from Yahoo! Movies. Ventura details from BrainyEncylopedia.com. Bergen details from "Candice Bergen: More Than 'Murphy,'" CBSNews.com, Jan. 24, 2003; IMDb. Midler details from All Music Guide.

p. 168-169: Stat from "Five Year Survival Rates," U.S. Census, April 1996; stat is middle mortality assumption in 2000-2005 for people ages 40-44 living to ages 45-49. Godspeed!

Some quotes were first uncovered on the website Bartleby.com.

HANKERING FOR MORE?

 99% can't wait to take the "How 40 Are You?" interactive quiz

 100% plan to send free 40th birthday e-cards to friends

 101% are dying for the scoop on other landmark ages, like 50

ACKNOWLEDGMENTS

Thanks to the terrific Lisa Bankoff
and Tina DuBois, and our undying
gratitude to the Crown BOA squad:
Annik La Farge and Mario Rojas.

Also, thanks to all of our friends,
whom we didn't have to bother nearly
as much about this one as we did
about the last one.

Special thanks to our families for the
best 40 years of our lives (projected).
Also, JVG thanks Xina, because he
does. Again. And Josh thanks Roslyn.

JOSHUA ALBERTSON, LOCKHART STEELE, and **JONATHAN VAN GIESON** have created or produced a variety of media projects. The first book in this series, *Book of Ages 30,* was published in 2003. They live in New York City.

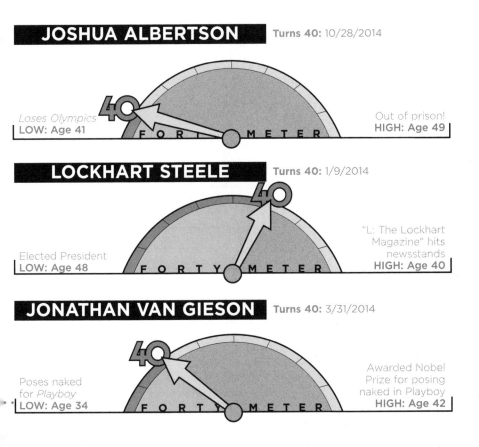

JOSHUA ALBERTSON
Turns 40: 10/28/2014

Loses Olympics
LOW: Age 41

F O R T Y M E T E R

Out of prison!
HIGH: Age 49

LOCKHART STEELE
Turns 40: 1/9/2014

Elected President
LOW: Age 48

F O R T Y M E T E R

"L: The Lockhart Magazine" hits newsstands
HIGH: Age 40

JONATHAN VAN GIESON
Turns 40: 3/31/2014

Poses naked for *Playboy*
LOW: Age 34

F O R T Y M E T E R

Awarded Nobel Prize for posing naked in Playboy
HIGH: Age 42

Autographs

Autographs

IF YOU'RE
THIRTY

. . . you've already lost 10 percent of your muscle mass, and, on average, you're almost $20,000 in debt. But don't despair. At thirty, Harrison Ford was working as a carpenter, and neither Oprah nor Jane Austen had found fame. Edvard Munch's famous painting "The Scream"? Created at thirty. And, most heartening, you're still gettin' it on—2.24 times a week.

These are but a few of the factoids, demographic stats, quotes, biographical sketches, and sage and not-so-sage observations in this illustrated celebration of a landmark birthday and the decade that follows. Featuring everything you ever wanted to know about your thirties—and a few things you probably didn't—*Book of Ages 30* offers a chance to reflect on past accomplishments, look ahead to future successes, and completely freak out—all at the same time. . . . .

HOW DO YOU STACK UP?

BOOK OF AGES 30

JOSHUA
ALBERTSON
LOCKHART
STEELE
JONATHAN
VAN GIESON

Book of Ages 30
1-4000-5013-8
$13.95 (Canada: $21.00)

Available from Crown Publishers wherever books are sold.
www.crownpublishing.com